OPEN-MINDED EDUCATION

HOW TO DO WHAT YOU LOVE AND MAKE MILLIONS

NATHAN & JOSHUA GEWONDJAN

NEED HELP DISCOVERING YOUR PASSION?

Scan this QR code for some tips!

This book is dedicated to ...

the dreamers around the world.

"If you can dream it, you can do it."

—— *Walt Disney*

CONTENTS

INTRODUCTION—THE DREAM

ONE DREAM. ONE LOVE. ONE LIFE. No more, no less. That's what we've all been given. What's yours? What will you do with it?

What if we said you can do anything? You'd probably think we're crazy, right? We don't blame you. Humor us for a second. What if there were no limits on what you can be, do, and have? Who would you be? What would you do? What would you have?

It can be both scary and exciting to think about these questions as they relate to you. If you aren't sure how you'd answer all of these, that's ok. By the time you finish this book, you will have a much clearer picture on your own passions and desires and the road to living them.

We believe everyone has a dream. Everyone has a passion in one form or another. For some, it may be the feeling you get when you serve someone. For others, it could be music or acting. Then again, there are others who love to build things with their hands. There is no right or wrong dream. Our sole purpose and intent in writing this book is to help you bring your passions to the surface. We want you to believe in yourself and your future more than before you read this book.

Dreams are born, and although they may fade under suppression, lack of faith, perseverance, or drive, they never die. The important thing is to feed the flame of your dreams by thinking and acting in accordance with such a passion. In order to make this happen, you may need to think differently than you've ever thought before. That's why the name of this book is *Open-Minded Education*—because in order to reach your greatest potential, you've got to be free from thinking there's only one way of doing things. Anything is possible when you have a clear intention and a free mind.

If you want to achieve a specific end result, you must follow a specific way of acting and thinking. There is an endless amount of dreams and passions, but the laws in getting there are the same. The only change is the content of your thoughts and actions.

In this book, we begin with a brief history of the public education system in the United States, including its origins and how it's changed over time. Not many people know, or have been taught, how it came to be, how it's changed, or the intentions of the individuals who formed it. History, when taught correctly and internalized, can be one of the most interesting, applicable, and therefore enjoyable subjects one can study.

You'll also find a variety of tools you can use to strengthen your mindset so you may become the person who lives the life of their dreams. The outlook and attitude you maintain and sustain toward your circumstances and what you perceive as possible has everything to do with where you land. When you change your mind, you change your life. Even the small changes make a big difference.

When your mind is in the right place, you're open to learn and implement the necessary concepts to propel you toward achieving success. Such concepts include but aren't limited to finding a mentor, forming a mastermind group, and becoming self-educated to achieve success without obtaining an extensive and expensive formal education.

As a side note, you will notice portions of various chapters designated as personal experiences from co-writer Nathan. The intent in sharing these experiences is to make it a bit more real and concrete in order for you to see how it's possible for you to undergo such life changing events. Although they are Nathan's experiences, the concepts taught are fully endorsed by both writers.

Our hope is that even after necessary changes are made to the public education system, you will continue to live by the principles learned in this book throughout your life. Much of what is taught in this book are core principles that will improve the quality of your life. In other words, we're saying that if everything in the education system is suddenly fixed, learning and living the ideas taught herein will allow you to think outside the box and live your dreams.

Opening your mind to doing and thinking unconventionally can be a difficult and painful process, but we assure you it is rewarding like no other. The process of identifying and unlocking your full potential is both invigorating and energizing. Buckle up. Take a breath, and get ready to open your mind!

PART I

CONVENTIONAL EDUCATION

1

THE HISTORY OF THE PUBLIC EDUCATION SYSTEM

"Those that fail to learn from history are doomed to repeat it."

-Winston Churchill

Those words by Winston Churchill disturbed me just a bit. I read them as I waited to take the Scholastic Aptitude Test (SAT), a standardized examination required for admission into the university I planned to attend. It was an early morning, especially for a Saturday. I was never one for taking tests but knew that if I wanted to attend college, this was the way. As I mused over the quote on the wall, I had a feeling that even though we were repeating these words many times to the point of becoming a cliché, we were not internalizing the important principle shared by Mr. Churchill. I thought to myself that unless a change is made, we're headed for a future with the same plot as seen throughout the course of history despite the use of this common phrase time and time again.

FIRST THINGS FIRST, IF WE ARE GOING TO LEARN FROM HISTORY and not seal ourselves to the inevitable fate of repeating it, we must learn and understand history as it really happened. Would you enjoy hearing your friend tell a story about you and completely butcher the entire thing? From the beginning to end, the story changes and evolves to the point that every aspect, both major and minor, is hardly recognizable by the protagonist (you). You would not appreciate this very much. Similarly, think of those who have come before us and the things they've done, both good and bad. It would be unjust to discredit, taint, pollute, dilute, or falsify these stories in any way. In addition, the golden rule states: "Do unto others as you would have them do unto you."

The concept of changing history to fit your point of view has grown in popularity over the more recent years and appears to be an ongoing trend. Our intent is to give you a breather from what appears to be the new norm of alterations in history and tell it like it really happened. That being said, let's take a brief look at the history of the public school system based on the facts and not through the lens of alteration or modification.

Timeline of the Public School System in the United States

After much study and research, we have identified some key events and dates pertaining to the history of the public school system in the United States. Seeing these to be of utmost importance for learning and understanding from our history, we've included this information for your benefit. This timeline is by no means comprehensive and does not contain every historical event regarding the acceptance of each school based on status, sex, race, or other factor. However, it does contain all the essential information to get a clear picture on the origin and evolution of the public school system in the United States of America.

1600s

The earliest records we have tell of schools opening in the 13 colonies during the 17th century. The Puritans valued education more than most, which led to a higher literacy rate than many other countries. Educational opportunities were prevalent but not as prominent in the southern colonies due to their more rural nature. Much of the education and instruction received in the south at that time was found in mentorships and private tutors.

|

1635

The Boston Latin School opened and was considered the first public school in the United States. To this day, it remains the oldest public school in the nation. Initially, the school was funded by donations and land rentals. As the name implies, the primary subject taught at the school was Latin. In addition to instructing students to read and write in Latin, this institution's goal was to prepare its students for college. It may be worthy to note that Benjamin Franklin attended and dropped out of the Boston Latin School.

|

1639

The first taxpayer supported school in North America opens. This school was known as the Mather School. The primary subjects taught were both reading and writing in

English, Latin, and several other languages. This was the birth of free education in the United States.

1647

The Massachusetts Bay Colony concluded that every town of 50 people should have an elementary school while towns of 100 people should be equipped with a school of Latin. Students were taught how to read primarily so they could read and understand the Bible. Basic religious information and principles were also a point of study in these early schools.

|

1700s

During the 18th century, the majority of schools were either a private and/or religious institution. Most public schools that had been developed previously had been transformed or replaced by private schools during this era. Family, community, and religion were at the core of the curriculum taught. This is primarily attributed to the fact that the majority of the early settlers in America were extremely religious and understood and knew the importance of not only learning these virtues but also applying them on a daily basis.

|

1779

Thomas Jefferson proposes a two-track educational system for "the labored and the learned" in which scholarships would allow few of the laboring class to advance. In his own words, he said it was a process of "raking a few geniuses from the rubbish."

1789

The Continental Congress (prior to the ratification of the United States Constitution) passed a law creating "townships," reserving a portion of each township for a local school. These "land grants" later became what is known as "land grant universities," which was the start of the state public universities we see across the nation today.

|

1790

The Pennsylvania state constitution calls for free public education for poor children funded by citizens of the state who could afford to fund it not only for their own children but for other families' children as well.

|

1805

New York Public School Society was formed by wealthy businessmen to provide education for poor children. Schools are run on the "Lancasterian" system in which one "master" (teacher) instructs hundreds of students at a time. The older students then pass the information down to younger students. The principles emphasized in this new system included obedience and discipline—both qualities that factory owners wanted in their workers.

1817

A petition is presented at a Boston Town meeting for the establishment of free public primary schools. Businessmen, local merchants, and wealthier artisans become the main supporters of such primary schools. Many wage earners opposed the petition due to the additional taxes levied against them.

|

1820

The first public high school opens in the United States.

|

1827

Massachusetts passes a law to provide all grades of public schooling open to every student free of charge.

|

1837

Horace Mann becomes secretary of the Massachusetts Board of Education. At which time, he resigned from all other business and professional occupations and spent the majority of his time in the education field. Mann had many friends with political power, including those in the Whig Party. He persuaded them to create laws in favor of tax-supported schools and education. Mann was responsible for much of the educational reform seen in the 1800s.

Another noteworthy milestone that took place in 1837 was the actions of a major industrialist, Edmund Dwight. He claimed a State Board of Education to be so important to factory owners that he offered to provide it with extra money of his own in its support.

|

1846–1856

Ireland experienced the potato famine, which resulted in many individuals traveling to the U.S. This led to more than 1.5 million people immigrating to America in this decade. Many of the immigrants were of a different faith than that of those already settled in the USA. This created a considerable amount of unrest and tension due to the religious principles taught in the schooling system at the time. After some time, new private schools began to form by those of the same faith as the Irish immigrants.

During this decade, the industry leaders had a continuously growing need for obedient and docile workers. They relied on the public school system to produce such individuals.

|

1852

The State of Massachusetts becomes the first state to pass the compulsory school attendance act, making it mandatory to attend school. This was designed to make sure the poor immigrants were civilized, disciplined, and obedient to avoid social upheaval.

1890s

These years marked the beginning of the Progressive Era and the Progressive Reform of the school system led by John Dewey. This era birthed the idea that a child should be taught to reach its full potential and be an active participant in a democratic society with a progressive education.

|

1900

By this time, 34 states had some type of compulsory school attendance act in place for children 8–14 years of age.

|

1902

A group of businessmen and politicians form the General Board of Education. The Rockefeller family donated $180 million in support of this newly organized group.

|

1918

Elementary school becomes mandatory in every state within the United States of America. At this time, government efforts shifted from the primary schools to higher level education by marketing loan programs, scholarships, and university education to students. This has proven to shape Americans' view of education for generations.

1920s

Sex education is introduced in high schools.

|

1932

Many schools reveal they have been using standardized intelligence testing to separate students into various academic tracks and programs.

|

1945

Following World War II, the G.I. Bill of Rights gave thousands of working-class men scholarships to attend college.

|

1956

The Massachusetts Higher Education Assistance Corporation (MHEAC) starts a guaranteed student loan program in the state of Massachusetts. This program insured students' bank loans with money raised through philanthropic donations from local businesses.

1958

The first federal loan program, the National Defense Student Loan (now the Perkins Loan), was created.

|

1962

In response to the case of Engel v. Vitale, the U.S. Supreme Court declares school-sponsored prayer unconstitutional.

|

1965

The first Higher Education Act (HEA) creates Guaranteed Student Loans (GSL), forming a public-private partnership with the federal government subsidizing capital from banks to provide loans to low- and mid-income students.

|

1972

The HEA Reauthorization Act creates the Student Loan Marketing Association (later known as Sallie Mae), to add liquidity to the GSL program by buying loans from lenders to provide more capital. This act also provided incentives for states to establish loan guarantee agencies, insuring federal student loans made by lenders.

1978

The Middle-Income Student Assistance Act (MISAA) eliminates the income restrictions for student loans, thus allowing middle- and high-income students to qualify for loans.

|

1980

The PLUS program was created to allow parents to borrow money on behalf of their children's education as part of the 1980 HEA Reauthorization.

|

1981

The MISAA is repealed by the Omnibus Reconciliation Act, which replaced the PLUS program with Auxiliary Loans to Assist Students (ALAS) and extended borrowing to graduate and independent undergraduate students. The Omnibus Reconciliation Act also imposed borrower loan origination fees on new student loans.

|

1986

The 1986 HEA Reauthorization splits the ALAS into the Supplemental Loan to Students (SLS) for graduate and independent students and brings back PLUS loans for parents.

1992

Direct lending is introduced through a program that makes unsubsidized loans available to every student. Annual and aggregate borrowing limits on PLUS loans are removed. Stafford and PLUS loans are restructured into the Federal Family Education Loan Program (FFEL).

|

2001

President George W. Bush signed the Economic Growth and Tax Relief Reconciliation Act to make student loan payments tax-deductible for borrowers.

|

2010

The FFEL is repealed by the Health Care and Education Responsibilities Act (HCERA). This made it so all new federal student loans (except for Perkins Loans) are made directly from the government to students.

Another noteworthy event that occurred this year was the implementation of the plan known as the Common Core Standards Initiative. This initiative adjusted the way certain topics were taught in the classroom and established high academic standards in subjects such as mathematics, English language arts, and literacy.

2014

22 states mandate sex education while 11 more mandate HIV education.

Horace Mann and the Prussian Education System

During Horace Mann's time on the school board beginning back in 1837, he prioritized making visits to various nations in Europe to analyze their education system. He took special interest in the schools in Prussia, a prominent state in Germany. He admired the way children were taught the same concepts in the same way, providing a common learning experience. Through such teaching methods, students were taught the same way regardless of talents, abilities, location, interests, or passions. This system of education works best when there is one group of directors or leaders making sure the material is uniform across the board.

The curriculum taught learners basic educational concepts such as mathematics, reading, and writing. There was also a healthy mix of principles such as obedience, duty to country, and general ethics.

The Prussian education system was developed in the 18th century. It consisted of eight mandatory years of basic education in which all community members must attend. This mandate was made possible for all students, whether rich or poor, due to the local taxpayer funding the entire school system. Following the required eight years of schooling, students were encouraged to attend secondary schools. This additional schooling was a personal expense, and not everyone attended.

In many ways, the Prussian system defined what to think, how long to think about it, and when to think about something else. The order and organization of such a system is quite marvelous. When such a structure is followed, every student receives the same education experience regardless of circumstances or history.

Side Effects of The Prussian Education System

One of the major side effects of the Prussian educational system is that one group or agency typically holds the majority of power in determining the concepts taught and the methods used in teaching them. As we'll cover in a later chapter, it's always better to diversify the amount of power and control given to a specific person or group. With some study of history, we learn the nature of human beings to be that when even a small amount of power is obtained, as they may suppose, they seek for more and more until it utterly consumes and quite unfortunately corrupts them. Giving a select group control of what and how the rising generation learns can limit the open-mindedness of the people in the long run.

This lack of open-mindedness often passively limits the student's freedom to choose which paths they would take in their educational journey. History and experience have shown that the Prussian model of education is primarily designed to create two types of people: employees and soldiers. These are both reputable directions to go in life, but the balance is lacking. Again, the side effect is conditioning the mind to think a certain way while lacking the ability and skill to think open mindedly.

You may have noticed some similarities in the Prussian and United States education systems. Obviously, it's not identical, but when you take the time to learn about both, the similarities are evident. Mann may have had good intentions when he sought to reform the educational system in the United States to conform with that of Prussia, but it is highly unlikely he envisioned the long-term narrow-minded effects of his actions.

Altogether, there are valuable lessons to be learned from the concepts and principles taught within the Prussian model of education as well as the implementation of the school system itself. With these lessons learned in our minds and hearts, we must always stay aware of true success and be accepting of alternative methods in achieving such a feat. Of all the side effects caused by the Prussian's teaching methods, the overall theme is a "one size fits all" approach to education. Although on many occasions, "one size fits [most]," there will consistently be those who do not thrive under this model. By learning the history of the United States public education system and those of other countries, we're more prepared to hedge against the undesired outcome so elegantly stated by Winston Churchill in the beginning of this chapter. Then, and only then, will we become better prepared to take responsibility for paving the way to a better future of inclusiveness and acceptance.

2

THE STATE OF THE SYSTEM

"The function of education, therefore, is to teach one to think intensively and to think critically. But education which stops with efficiency may prove the greatest menace to society. The most dangerous criminal may be the man gifted with reason, but with no morals."

-Martin Luther King, Jr.

AS WE SAW IN THE PREVIOUS CHAPTER, THE EDUCATION SYSTEM in the United States of America has evolved in great measure over the years. This change can be seen in many ways, but in order to determine if public education in its current form is right for us or our children, we need to pause and examine the current state of the system.

Just as one may determine the health of a business by reviewing the numbers and data on the balance sheet, so it is with the health of the education system. We learn the health and effectiveness of public schools with certain studies and results shown by notable sources and organizations. Let's jump right in!

According to the National Center for Education Statistics, the average amount of school days in the year comes out to 180 with each school day at a length of 6.7 hours.[1] Do the math. That's a grand total of an average of 1,206 hours each year.

Keep in mind these statistics don't include the amount of time spent with school sponsored extracurricular sports, clubs, and activities. After-school programs such as these can and often do enrich the lives of those who participate, however, it does take a chunk of time. The average practice time for high school sports is anywhere from 10 to 12 hours each week, which comes out to about two hours each school day.

When you take these and add homework to the mix, things get dicey. The amount of homework given out to students whether in elementary, middle, or high school is considerable, especially on the high school level. A recent study conducted by the University of Phoenix College of Education surveyed 1,000 K-12 teachers and found, among other things, that high schoolers receive an average of 3.5 hours of homework each week per class.[2] For high school students who are taking five classes, that's up to 17.5 hours of homework per week.

There is value in all of these things, but not much matters if you aren't getting enough sleep. Based on a study conducted by the American Academy of Sleep Medicine, the Center for Disease Control and Prevention (CDC) recommended that children between the ages of 13-18 sleep for 8-10 hours for optimal health. They also stated that getting enough sleep can minimize the ever more prevalent behavioral and attention span problems found in students.[3] The CDC also analyzed data from the 2015 national and state Youth Risk Behavior Surveys in which students were asked how much sleep they got on school nights. This study showed that 72.7% of high school students did not get adequate sleep.[4] If we consider the fact that the human brain isn't fully developed until well into your

20's, which has been proven in a number of studies, the amount of sleep a child receives every day has a big impact on their state of being both now and in the future. Sleep should never be, but oftentimes is, sacrificed to compensate for extra time needed in other areas of life.

Based on these studies, let's break it down and see what a day in the life of the average high schooler looks like. If they are spending an average of 30 minutes to get ready and eat breakfast, 6.7 hours in class, 2.5 hours for after-school activities, 1 hour for travel (30 minutes both to and from school), 3.5 hours of homework, 1 hour for dinner, and 9 hours for sleeping, if we do the math, it comes to a grand total of 24.2 hours.

Most of these numbers are a little on the high end. For example, when was the last time a high school student got 9 hours of sleep or spent 3.5 hours each day on homework? Most of them don't, but just because they don't, doesn't mean they shouldn't. That being said, the point is, when you fill each day with busy work, there is next to no time to live a free life.

If we compare a school day for children to a day at work for a 9-5 employee, there isn't a whole lot of difference. Is this a coincidence? Not likely. As we saw over the course of history, the public education system was formed and influenced most by those of great wealth. Thus, they found it fitting to instill the standard daily schedule in each of their future potential employees. They needed a way to ensure they would have a steady flow of respectable personnel to keep their business growing. This makes sense from a business standpoint but could be considered wrong from a moral standpoint. You decide.

When your day is structured the same way every day for years, especially from an incredibly young age, you become accustomed to the known and predictable, which leads to your creative energy becoming and often remaining dormant and untapped. We all have 24 hours in a day. No more, no less. In a world where everything is increasingly faster-paced and adults are already overworking themselves, do we want to pass this down to our children?

Based on the facts and statistics previously stated, the Prussian school system and therefore the United States school system serve as a place of learning and understanding to a degree, but, whether intentional or unintentional, undoubtedly serve as a place of conditioning and training. In the workforce, you have managers, CEOs, and presidents. In the classroom, you have teachers, principals, and members of the board of education. Schools are places of training and conditioning for the workforce.

In the current system of education, teachers and principals have little influence on the curriculum taught in their classroom or schoolhouse. In fact, if they veer off the assigned material too much, disciplinary action is enforced, and they will likely be replaced depending on the extent to which they deviate. Teachers and principals are hired to teach and enforce school curriculum and policies, just as managers are hired to enforce and teach policies within a business.

K-12 schools aren't the only ones who have adopted many of the Prussian's ways of educating. Upon examination, we find many of the same principles and techniques perpetuated on the collegiate and university level as well. As you may have experienced, there are some changes when going to college, but the majority of the school structure and teaching methods remain unchanged.

One of the few differences found in the transition from high school to college is that you now have the choice of which major and emphasis to focus on. The majority of colleges still have certain required classes that must be taken prior to graduation; the classes we refer to are often called "general education." These courses vary from school to school but share many similarities across the board, hence the term "general." All of this being said, the majority of classes taken on the university level are based on your choice of major, which is quite refreshing.

The biggest difference, however, is that in contrast to the free, tax-dollar supported public education received from kindergarten to the senior year of high school, you are now required to pay for your college education experience unless, that is, you're able to acquire financial aid by means of the government, college, or other organization. Nonetheless, payment is expected and must be paid if you are to attend a college or university.

Over time, we have seen the price, and therefore debt accrued through the expense of colleges and universities, increase in great measure (See figure 1). A contributor to the increase in price for an education on the university or college level could likely be the concept of financing. There is no question, the ability to finance college tuition gave access to those who previously appeared to be hopeless in funding a college degree. Nevertheless, the fact remains, when you give someone the ability to finance an item such as a car, house, boat, or college education, it will **always** cost more. This is because you're not only paying the principal amount, but you are also paying the price to borrow the money, or in other words, the interest.

By providing the item to you earlier than if you were to save up for it and pay cash on the spot, the lender asks in return for a greater amount of money paid in the end. Financing is just another way to provide an additional service to the customer, but, in order for it to be a win-win transaction between both the lender and the borrower, more money will need to be spent on the borrower's end to make up for the opportunity cost of cash on the lender's side. It's not bad to finance an item or even an education. This is just one of many reasons the price for a college education has increased over time and is so expensive today.

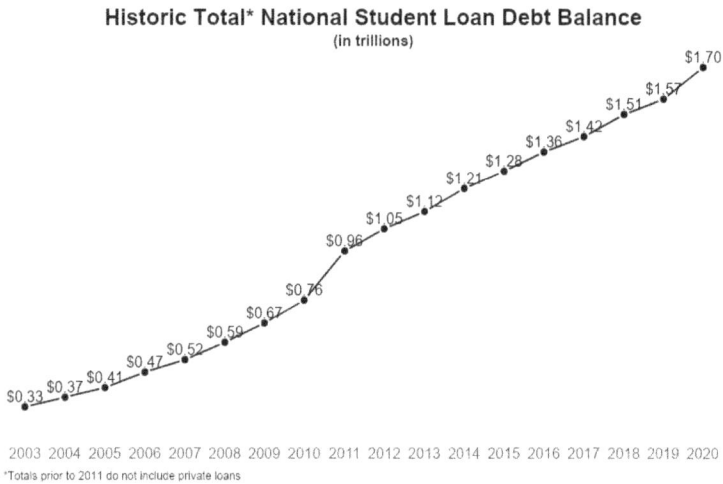

(Figure 1 provided by www.educationdata.org)

The history of student loans is fascinating. As discussed in the previous chapter, we have seen them evolve from being held primarily by private banks and lenders to the current state where the majority is held and controlled by the federal government. We may draw a parallel as we remember the history of the public school system. Just as we saw the public school system change from the local and private nature with which it was born, so too, we have seen in more recent years, the student loan invention altered to appease the appetite for control we find in governmental agencies.

As seen in Figure 1, student loan debt in the United States now totals over $1.5 trillion. Yes, that's correct—more than $1.5 trillion! It has also been reported that student debt grows

6 times faster than the nation's economy. 92.6% of this whopping sum is held by undergraduates who have borrowed money from the federal government. When we take an average of this number, each of these students owe approximately $36,510 in federal loans.

Another insight comes from a study performed by New York Life in 2019. They polled 2,200 adults about their financial mistakes and discovered that the average participant reported taking 18.5 years to pay off their student loans.[5] That means, on average, if someone were to take out a loan for college at the age of 22, they wouldn't pay it off until the age of 40. This may be a contributing factor to why most people don't start retirement planning until 10+ years after they have been working on paying down their student loans.

Time is everything, and if nothing else, student loans can rob you of this hot commodity. The time in which you could be contributing to certain funds, employing the phenomenon which Einstein refers to as "the 8th wonder of the world," could be lost forever with a rash, close-minded decision to follow the crowd. That's why it's so important to not procrastinate the day in which you plan and act to achieve your goals. We'll be going a bit more in depth in Chapter 8 on investing and the effect of starting this "8th wonder" working for you from a young age.

We don't advocate against student loans and, quite frankly, find them to be incredibly useful for those who desire to attend college and lack the means. Nonetheless, be sure you know what you're doing before you do it. Take a few precious hours to learn about what is involved so you can save yourself years of regret down the road.

Despite the current state of the education system, the future has never been brighter. Opportunities for education are more accessible now than ever before in the history of mankind.

With the technological updates, one can learn anything, anywhere, at any time. Overcoming the obstacle of ignorance isn't difficult but does take effective use of the tools with which we've been given. In the day in which we live, ignorance is a choice.

---

1. Schools and Staffing Survey—https://nces.ed.gov/surveys/sass/tables/sass0708_035_s1s.asp
2. Stainburn, Samantha. (February 27, 2014). "High Schools Assign 3.5 Hours of Homework a Night, Survey Estimates." https://www.edweek.org
3. "Sleep in Middle and High School Students." (Reviewed September 10th, 2020). https://cdc.gov
4. See footnote 3.
5. Hecht, Anna. (October 29, 2019). "Study shows financial regret is real—and this mistake can take an average 18.5 years to recover." https://www.cnbc.com

---
3

OPENING THE MIND

"If education doesn't solve a problem, then it is a problem; If the educated do not solve problems, then they are the problems."

-*Ernest Agyemang Yeboah*

WE BELIEVE EDUCATION TO BE OF UTMOST IMPORTANCE AS FAR as it is done in the right way and for the right reasons. There is no replacement for intellectual development and such ought to be a lifelong endeavor. Unfortunately, over time and in its current form, education in the United States has become widely known as attending a government subsidized organization in which all material and curriculum taught must fit a predetermined criterion decided upon by a group of political leaders. In great measure, due to the implementation of the Prussian school system in the United States (an endeavor led by Horace Mann as discussed previously), education has become a means of teaching others how to be in order to produce outcomes sought after by business leaders and wealthy individuals. This process begins at an early age, therefore making it difficult to have a truly open mind.

Education is more than just attending an organized institution and a graduation ceremony.

Although most people experience the public education system from kindergarten to high school, many recognize the one-sided and close-minded view in which many of us see education. In light of this, we've put together a list of things that would allow the students to exit the system with a bit more of an open mind and much more prepared to face the challenges of life. We believe these would improve the effectiveness of public education overall.

TEACH ESSENTIAL TOPICS FOR LIFE SUCCESS

The first thing we suggest to improve the overall effectiveness of public education is the inclusion of various topics that are immediately useful in achieving practically every students' goals beyond high school. Some of these include: time management, how and when to use debt, the effects of inflation, and other basic financial knowledge.

We recognize that schools do teach an amount of financial knowledge such as budgeting, balancing a checkbook, etc., but these are for consumers. If you want to be financially free and have some additional free time to pursue your dreams, financial intelligence is non-negotiable. If some students prefer not to learn these things, they should have the option to decline the opportunity. However, this doesn't change the fact that these topics ought to be at least offered in a student's learning experience with the intent to help them achieve their goals and ambitions in life.

ENCOURAGE ADDITIONAL PARENTAL/FAMILY INVOLVEMENT

Remember how we talked about public education shifting from private to public? This shift perpetuated the decline of family involvement. This being said, we still see a decent amount of opportunities for the parents to play a role in the schooling experience. Some of these include: visiting their children at lunch, volunteering for various organizations and associations, and attending parent teacher conferences. However, despite all of this, parents aren't able to actively teach their children in the classroom. Admittedly, many parents are not qualified nor would they want to teach their children certain topics. With this in mind, it's nice the public schools offer to teach students these and other topics, because without them, the kids may not have had the opportunity to learn much at all. We must remember still, there is a balance in all things. Some parents are, quite frankly, more qualified to teach a certain topic than the teacher at the school. In this case, if the parent chooses to, there ought to be an option for the parent to take a greater role in the teaching of said topic in class.

A teacher's role is critical in the development of a young person but can never trump the God-given role of a parent. Problems arise when students spend more time with teachers at school rather than meaningful time in the home. The extended amount of time spent with school officials creates a need for additional material taught in the classroom. A couple of these are life skills and sex education. Ideally, these things, and others, should be taught primarily in the home by people who love those whom they're teaching, all the while allowing the students to learn and be whomever they decide to be.

We realize that many students aren't fortunate enough to have both parents in the home or maybe they don't even have one. It's quite possible that there's a dysfunctional relationship on one or both sides. Nevertheless, that doesn't take away from the divine role parents play in raising their children and the astounding influence they can have on their learning experience. So, whether you are having problems with, don't have, or never had parents who care about you, decide now to be the change, and start a new trend.

Teach and Incentivize a Balance of Virtues

As was discussed in Chapter 1, when wealthy businessmen gained control of the education system and Horace Mann discovered the Prussian education model, adjustments were made to implement certain principles these individuals thought to be of great worth in molding and developing the right type of employees within their companies. Some of these concepts include obedience, docility, and standardization.

These principles in and of themselves are valuable things to learn and apply. They have their place on the road to becoming great. In addition, if you study those who have accomplished big things, you'll find that they possessed and adhered to many similar principles at one time or another.

What, then, is the problem with teaching and incentivizing these specific virtues and behaviors in school? The answer is: absolutely nothing! Many lessons we learn in school are invaluable. Issues arise when an overemphasis is placed on these principles rather than balancing all the essentials and allowing the student to decide which ones to focus on for the achievement of their goals. In certain professions, some skills are used more than others. For example, an entrepreneur, most of the time, doesn't have a standardized way of building a company. There are laws and concepts that must be abided by that will allow success and profitability to come quicker than others. Contrast that with a soldier. A soldier must have a standardized way of doing things in order to ensure the safety of the people and success of the mission. Neither one is bad, in fact, both are needed to keep society intact. The point is, when you have a good mixture of different attributes and qualities, it is easier to decide which path you will take because there is no bias or trained skillset one way or another.

This principle is expounded upon so beautifully in the analogy of the two wolves given by Billy Graham. In his book *The Holy Spirit: Activating God's Power in Your Life*, he writes that we all have two wolves inside of us, one being good and the other evil in nature. He elaborates on the concept and concludes by making the point that the one we feed will always prevail. Thus, if the principles being taught and demonstrated in school are tailored to becoming an employee or a soldier, you can't expect the entrepreneurial, artistic, creative thinking wolf inside you to come out on top.

Students should be encouraged to learn and study entrepreneurial, artistic, and creative thinking principles inside and outside of the classroom in addition to the virtues already being taught. If public education is to improve and we are to become more open minded, there must be an unbiased presentation of all virtues, both those geared towards employees and those of entrepreneurs—therefore, allowing every student the power to choose for themselves which wolf gets the grub.

Promote Creativity

The word "education" is derived from two Latin roots: *educare*, which means to train or to mold. While the other, *educere*, means to draw out or to lead out. Thus, education is a blend between training and drawing out from within. One may say then that the meaning of "educating" someone is to provide them with the training necessary to draw out what is already within them.

Education is not merely the art of filling one's head with a variety of facts, but rather, the pursuit of developing the faculties of the mind, which include imagination, perception, intuition, memory, will, and reason. Most everyone has them. However, just because you have them does not mean you're using them. I'm sure you've heard people say, "I'm just not a creative person," or "I'm terrible at remembering names." Although it is true that some have a stronger memory, intuition, or imagination than others, this is only the case due to the amount of time dedicated to improving and strengthening these mental "superpowers."

Just as your biceps get weaker when not strengthened through exercise on a regular basis, so too, your mental faculties become progressively weaker as they are neglected. Neither physical nor mental exercises are easy, but you always feel better once you've done them. The development of your creative mind begins at an early age. When a child is young, they are encouraged to be creative and imaginative. They live in a world in which they are the creators. Unfortunately, when these children begin attending school, they soon learn the effects of the use of these faculties in the classroom or with their homework assignment. Most people don't recognize these things as "using your imagination" or "thinking outside the box." They are more commonly known as "not paying attention" or "not following instructions." As a result, learners receive disciplinary action, humiliation, and/or another form of punishment for use of such things.

In school, you are dictated what to think (the required classes you need to graduate), when to think (6.7 hours a day, 180 days each year), and how long to think about it (until you hear the ding of the school bell).

TEACH PARENTS AND/OR STUDENTS TO PAY THE PRICE

When you pay for something yourself or work for it in one way or another, inherently, you will have a greater appreciation for it. This is such a simple concept but oftentimes isn't the most enjoyable to learn through experience. However, you can always tell those who have learned this principle from those who have not. We all know those kids who have everything handed to them on a silver platter who fit the textbook definition of the word "entitled." You know, the ones who have the crust cut off their peanut butter and jelly sandwiches by mommy or daddy because they didn't like the flavor.

Cutting the crust off your PB&J isn't bad, we even enjoy a sandwich without the crust from time to time, but kids should be taught how to do it and expected to effectively provide for themselves. It's the principle taught in the adage, "Give a man a fish, and you feed him for a day. Teach a man to fish, and you feed him for a lifetime." Self-reliance is the name of the game. If you'd like to learn more about how to avoid the attitude of entitlement and become more self-reliant, check out *Extreme Ownership* by Jocko Willink and Leif Babin. Willink and Babin share the life lessons they learned as United States Navy Seals in a manner that is truly inspiring. If you struggle with taking responsibility or making excuses, this book is a game changer.

Have you ever heard about the concept of "TANSTAAFL?" When spelled out, it means "there ain't no such thing as a free lunch." In old times, many saloons would offer a free lunch with the purchase of one alcoholic beverage. This was a marketing tactic. Following the purchase of the first alcoholic beverage and the consequent so-called "free lunch," additional beverages were often ordered, therefore providing the profits for the saloon.

Over time, the saying has been used by many well-known individuals such as Walter Morrow, Milton Friedman, Richard Maybury, and Robert Heinlein. Each of these individuals recognized the principles one can derive therefrom. Napoleon Hill taught this principle when he said, "There is no such thing as something for nothing" in his book *Think and Grow Rich*. When something is offered by man, it is never without a cost. The price must always be paid whether in the form of time, money, or energy.

Most schools in the United States are subsidized by the government from tax-payers' dollars. One could then argue that it isn't free because they're already paying for it primarily through property taxes. Although there is some substance to that point, most people don't associate the payment of taxes with their children's education. If so, there would be much less hostility toward the government and paying these tariffs. Even though they are paying for a portion of their children's or their neighbor's children's education, they may as well not be. The first reason being that you don't have a choice unless you want to risk losing your property. The other reason is simply because the association of paying property taxes or rent rarely comes with the cost of the children's education in mind.

The effects of not realizing you're paying for something is essentially the same as if you weren't paying for it to begin with. This may be one of the reasons for an apathetic attitude towards education and disrespect for mentors and teachers as children get older. When children are young, parents should consciously pay for their kids' education. As children grow older, they ought to be taught how to contribute to the payment of their education in pursuit of abolishing the attitude of entitlement.

ENCOURAGE LEARNING THROUGH FAILURE

The suggestion we have for opening our minds to various methods of education is regarding failure. Learning through failure must be encouraged. What does it mean to fail? According to the Merriam-Webster Dictionary, the word "fail" means to fall short, to be unsuccessful, and to disappoint expectations or trust. To summarize, failure is the art of messing up.

In school, the knee-jerk reaction of punishing a student for not doing something a certain way (i.e., failing), has been effective in promoting the fear of failure. "Fear" is a four-letter word. Then again, so is "fail." Giving failure a negative connotation often leads to a lack or discouragement of trying and pursuing dreams.

To be clear, failure is not a happy event, nor should it be. We must learn to recognize it as a teaching event. None of us want to fail, but practically all of us want to learn and improve. The fastest way to do this is through learning from our mistakes (i.e., failure).

Failure is like a flesh-wound. It happens by accident, hurts for a while, and usually heals up within a couple weeks. At the moment, it hurts like no other, but depending on your perspective, it heals and becomes wisdom to guide your future in such a way as to not make the same mistakes again and again. Zig Ziglar put it this way when he said, "Failure is an event, not a person." Nobody is destined to be a failure. We will all inevitably fail at one, or likely many, times in our lives. Just remember that failure is a stepping stone to success.

The next time you fail, don't fret. If you fall for a bit, identify a lesson to be learned so you don't repeat the same mistake, dust yourself off, and keep moving forward. Look at failure as an opportunity to learn and improve instead of getting stuck in a downward spiral of negativity.

PROVIDE MORE EFFECTIVE METHODS OF TEACHING

Many people say nothing has changed in the education system for a long period of time. Although many aspects haven't changed, we politely disagree with this idea simply because there indeed have been several significant additions and adjustments to the topics discussed and programs implemented within the system, and we will continue to see it evolve in the future as we have in the past.

Notwithstanding the adjustments and implementations made to the system, the teaching and learning model employed has not changed enough or even at all since Horace Mann decided it would be a good idea to clone the Prussian education system in the United States. Certain topics may be an issue for some, but our primary focus is on the way it's being taught. It's like Mom used to say, "It's not what you said but how you said it."

What, then, is the right teaching method? The best answer to most questions (and this is no different) is it depends. The right teaching method depends on the student and their preferred style of learning. Everyone is unique and deserves the opportunity to learn in the way that best fits their needs. Many have recognized this point. Albert Einstein spoke of teaching to the needs of the student when he stated, "Everybody is a genius, but if you judge a fish by its ability to climb a tree, it will live its whole life believing that it is stupid."

In the larger scheme of things, there are certain teaching methods that have been proven to be more effective than others. Based on a study performed by the Proceedings of the National Academy of Sciences of the United States of America, students in **traditional lecture heavy** classes are 1.5 times less likely to retain the information taught compared to a class that uses more stimulating, active learning methods.[1]

Large class sizes make it near impossible for the instructor to work with each learner one-on-one for a personal learning experience. We refer to the second item in this chapter for the best remedy for this problem. What better way to provide a personalized teaching experience than through the people who typically know their children better than anyone—the parents!

As uncomfortable as it may be to admit, we need a change. With the many changes in the world today and the rate at which technology is advancing, we must all take a step back and find ways to become more open minded toward ourselves and others in regards to education. Change can be difficult to manage, especially when it's regarding something that has been so intertwined within our culture and lifestyle. The education system as we know it today has been struggling to provide students with the resources, knowledge, and skills necessary for living a truly wealthy life. A college education, although helpful, doesn't give the same advantage it once did. It must be supplemented with additional independent study to learn those topics of financial education, life skills, and everlasting principles that govern our lives. If you desire to become successful in achieving freedom in the fullest, truest sense of the word, college may, but does not have to be, at the top of your list of to-dos.

Because of the state of the system and the emphasis placed on attending a university, most people look at you differently when you tell them you're dropping out of college and pursuing alternative forms of education. When they hear you're planning on homeschooling your kids, you can almost hear that sudden movie-like vinyl stop sound effect in the background interrupting the pleasant music as the words leave your lips. Let that reaction be a sign that you're heading in the right direction. This is because you've made the choice to be different. You've decided to dive headfirst into the unknown and follow your heart. Don't look back. The unknown can be a scary place, and because of such, relatively few decide to take the walk. That's why people see it as different. Superficially, it will appear as though you are a reject or an outcast. This is when they secretly wish they had the courage to do what you've decided to do so badly they can't bear to be around you. Ask anyone who is going or has gone against the norm, and they'll tell you that the road to freedom can, at times, be a lonely one. Just remember, in the end, the view is always worth the climb.

Where do you want to end up? Do you want to work all your life for someone else's dreams? What are your dreams? Where do you see yourself in 5, 10, even 20 years down the road? Can you feel what it feels like to already have achieved that goal? Are you willing to do what it takes to make it a reality? Are you ready to undergo a paradigm shift?

Take some time to ponder and answer these questions. Your responses will determine the best course of action you should take. Be honest with yourself and the education you'll need to accomplish your goals. For those struggling to take hold to the idea that education doesn't have to be acquired in a classroom from a "qualified" teacher or instructor with a plethora of certifications and degrees, you're not alone. It takes many a considerable amount of time to accept this idea.

The paradigm shift must take place in the battlefield between your ears. The choice to open your mind is a rewarding and meaningful one. Such a choice allows you greater freedom and less fear, and you're able to take the lid off your dreams and not worry about what other people think. In the following pages, we'll be diving a little deeper into what makes a strong mindset and how we can fortify our mind to not only be able to make the shift in our view of education but to be mentally resilient and sound for the rest of our lives.

1. Proceedings of the National Academy of Sciences of the United States. "Active learning increases student performance in science, engineering and mathematics." (Published May 12th, 2014, edited June 10th, 2014).

PART II

A NEW STATE OF MIND

4

WEALTH MINDSET

"If you want to improve the quality of your life, start allocating a portion of each day to changing your paradigm."

-Bob Proctor

———

Many people often ask me if I've always had such strong feelings towards receiving a standard college education. My response usually leaves them baffled and awestruck. My answer is that "nobody had a more 'college is for everyone' attitude than I." My feelings were strong and poignant to the extent that my impression was that if someone decided not to attend a college or university, they had just doomed themselves to flip burgers their entire life. It was as if I had rewritten Patrick Henry's famous slogan "give me liberty or give me death" as "give me [a college education] or give me death." I'll admit, I was a pretty hard-headed and closed-minded kid.

During my first year in college, I was a member of the student representative council, new student mentor/tutor, model, and was involved in various other organizations on campus. So, what happened? What caused such a major shift? In a word: education.

After my freshman year of college, I took a couple years off for a two-year, religious, community service mission. At the end of my service, the COVID-19 pandemic had emerged and affected the whole world in major ways. I returned home some time before my expected date of arrival as a point of caution regarding the virus, at which time I proceeded to enroll in an assortment of online college classes.

To say I struggled with the distance learning experience is an understatement. This is coming from a guy who obtained his high school diploma online. Go figure! Call it weak, apathetic, lazy, maybe even short-sided, but at length, I concluded to drop all my courses except for one. This allowed me some extra free time to pursue other modes of study on topics of my choosing. During this additional time, I specifically studied the words and teachings of Bob Proctor, Robert Kiyosaki, Napoleon Hill, Douglas Andrew, and many other established authors on the topic of personal development and finance.

It was the study and application of this material that primed my brain for the paradigm shift. When I first heard the concept that the education system and colleges don't teach you how to be financially free, therefore perpetuating the survival mindset, I almost flipped. The concept seemed absurd and biased. How can that be the case?

After painfully questioning my way of thinking, I concluded that the only real bias was in between my ears. For a considerable amount of time, I was in disbelief and quite frankly didn't want to accept it. That idea went against my plans of living a chill, planned, simple life the way most people do. Only when I continued to think and ponder on the thought did it begin to take root and my understanding began to be enlightened. It's not a hard concept to teach or begin to understand once you see it work. The difficulty and discomfort come from displacing an old, familiar idea or paradigm and therefore begin believing the new idea.

If you find a concept to be difficult to mentally digest, dedicate some time to study and effort to apply. You will find and experience it first-hand. Anyone can tell you anything, but if you act on it, you gain the experience—the precursor to wisdom.

As human beings, we have the divinely appointed power to think and reason for ourselves. The American poet and writer Archibald MacLeish put it this way, "The only thing about a man that is a man ... is his mind. Everything else you can find in a pig or horse." This statement rings true. The ability to think is nothing to be taken lightly. We have our minds that we may learn the truth for ourselves. We believe that is one of the primary reasons we live on this earth: to learn and grow.

The way in which we think has a great deal to do with who we become and the quality of life we live. We're not just talking about material possessions, although they do play a role in all of this. There are other aspects pertaining to living a wealthy life of equal or even greater importance than the balance in your bank account. Some of these include your state of mind, relationships with family and friends, health, and your experiences. To live a wealthy life is to live an abundant life— which takes us to the difference between maintaining a lack or abundance mindset.

There are only two states of mind: lack and abundance. Each of us have experienced both at one time during our lives. To think abundantly is to live in a peaceful, unlimited, grateful, positive state of mind, which allows us to truly live, while a lack mindset can be identified by feeling worried, stressed, angry, limited, or essentially anything that the word "lack" implies. Let's discover what each of these looks like beginning with the lack mentality.

The Feeling of Lack

Every day we see people moving faster and faster, trying to get more of what appears as their piece of the pie. These actions stem from a lack mindset. What happens when you feel something is limited? You begin to worry and move fast because you feel that if you don't, the desired object or outcome will be snatched up by another.

This mindset has been paired with another described by Dr. Joe Dispenza as living in survival. We become subject to this state of being when we allow our environment to influence the way we feel, therefore altering our state of being. Dr. Dispenza elaborated on this point when he said, "If we cannot think beyond how we feel emotionally, then we are living according to what the environment dictates to our body. Rather than truly thinking, innovating, and creating, we merely fire the synaptic memories in other areas of our brain from our genetic or personal past; we instigate the same repetitive chemical reactions that have us living in survival mode."[1]

In the wild, when an animal is in danger, it puts all its focus and energy into resolving the dangerous situation through a method of either fighting or fleeing. These reactions are natural and instinctive. This is survival mode in action.

We, humans, have this same knee-jerk reaction when we perceive ourselves to be in physical or mental danger. Although, the difference between ourselves and all other wildlife as stated earlier by Archibald MacLeish, is our mind. With such, we have the ability to respond instead of react.

Reacting is acting without thinking while responding is stopping, thinking, then acting.

There have been a number of revolutionary discoveries in recent years in respect to the human mind, but we still know little about our true potential. The same power that allows us to respond in place of reacting, the mind, also allows us to call upon certain thoughts that drive our emotions. In other words, by controlling our thoughts, we can dictate the way we feel. Therefore, by thinking of a negative thought or experience, we can put ourselves in a lack mindset for an extended period of time even if the danger has long since passed.

In many cases, the long-term results of sustaining the lack mindset are disease and illness both mental and physical. Not only that, if we are giving all our energy to the emotions of lack, there will be nothing left to create the life we desire.

The Abundance Mindset

On the flip side, when you have and maintain an abundant mindset, you live as though there is more than enough to go around for everyone. Instead of worrying you may not get your piece of the pie, you resolve that you can just make a bigger pie, thereby benefiting everyone involved.

Abundance begins with the realization that everything originates from a flawless, higher intelligence. Some call this higher intelligence God, Buddha, The Universe, The Great Spirit, and several others. Regardless of your beliefs, you can live abundantly. However, if anything you associate with teaches anything contrary to such a notion, you may find it necessary to separate yourself therefrom in order to achieve your highest potential.

If we are to maintain an abundant state of mind, it is essential to understand that because everything originates from a perfect, higher power, it must, therefore, exist in unlimited quantities. We must see lack as an illusion and abundance as the unalterable truth. In a world where everyone has adopted and, at times, seems only to focus on appealing to the audience's emotions (a phenomenon referred to by Aristotle as Pathos), it is probable that this will require a shift in mindset. Based on the information regarding both the lack and abundance mindsets, take a moment and determine which one you find yourself living in most of the day. The first step in making a change is to recognize the need for it.

It has often been said that wherever you place your attention is inevitably where your energy flows. Similarly, when you focus on something, it grows. The question that remains then is what do you want to grow? Feelings of stress and survival or feelings of freedom and abundance? Which wolf will you feed?

Who do you want to be?

If we are to successfully make the shift from lack to abundance, we must put things into perspective. Working a 9-5 shift every business day for a meager income could be seen as simply living in survival. However, if you flip the coin over, you can see it as the perfect starting ground to building generational wealth. It's all relative. For some, working a full-time job as an employee for a long period of time is the best thing that could ever happen to them, but, then again, there are others that would rather die than work as an employee their entire lives. What do you prefer?

Becoming the Indispensable Employee

Depending on what you enjoy doing and the goals and vision you have in life, it would be worthwhile to consider traveling the road to being an indispensable employee. If you like the feeling of having a paycheck coming in on a frequent basis and not having to worry about covering overhead and payroll, the employee lifestyle might be your thing. In many ways, this is the easier route. This is the most traveled path, so there is less "off-roading" you'll have to do and plenty of great advice regarding how to land amazing jobs. You'll receive less criticism, take less risks, and hopefully be covered under your employer's health insurance plan.

When considering attending a four-year university or obtaining the required education through another means, keep in mind that it really depends on what you plan on doing with the education you obtain. For example, if you desire to become a doctor, lawyer, nurse, or mechanical engineer, studying and obtaining a degree from a major university may be the best option. However, in pursuit of considering all options, there are various trade schools, independent study courses, and apprenticeships that allow you to bypass the years of student loans and general knowledge that will most likely be forgotten with time. We'll elaborate on several different options in a later chapter.

The Life of an Entrepreneur/Investor

For those who desire a higher earning potential, want to be financially free, don't care what people think, enjoy being different, are willing to take a few more risks, and are thrilled with the idea of providing opportunities for those around them, you may want to consider entrepreneurship or becoming an investor. On this side of the coin, there is no cap on the amount of success you can achieve, but with no cap also comes no floor to a base salary or how far down you can fall. One could say there is no equalizer in the world of entrepreneurship and investing. The highs can be exhilarating, and the lows can be paralyzing.

The principles and methods expounded upon in this book benefit both employees and entrepreneurs but are especially beneficial for the latter. The biggest perk to becoming an investor or business owner is having the opportunity to become financially independent. That's not to say that every entrepreneur is financially free or it cannot be attained as an employee, but the chances of accomplishing this goal as an entrepreneur are much higher than any other route. Fortunately, and unfortunately, the only one to blame if it doesn't happen is the person you see when you look in the mirror.

Some may see less security in owning their own company. The biggest problem with security is it usually comes with the sacrifice of certain freedoms. We like to use the analogy of prison inmates to emphasize this principle. Those in prison have an immense amount of security, but on the flip side, the freedoms they enjoy are limited. Remember that in order to increase security, you may have to sacrifice certain freedoms you enjoy.

In terms of the best methods of becoming a business owner or investor, there are a plethora of options. Arguably one of the best things to do is to seek out and locate a mentor who is selfless enough to teach you what they know and help guide you along your journey. We will go more in depth on this topic in Chapter 6.

There are various schools and institutions that offer degrees and certifications in the entrepreneurial realm. These teach some good information and may provide some excellent networking opportunities but are not necessary to be a successful business owner. Some of your greatest resources will be carefully selected books, podcasts, YouTube videos, and several other forms of media. Start with identifying what you'd specifically like to learn, and make it happen. Take one step at a time, and keep moving forward.

Much can be said about the benefits of going to work every day to make a living as an employee, but think about that statement: "Make a living." Doesn't that just scream survival mindset? If an employee were to stop working, the paychecks would stop coming in, and they wouldn't be able to provide housing, food, and water for themselves or their family. The most abundant, selfless, and truly fulfilling thing you can do is work to learn and create flows of passive income so you can be free to live out your dreams and teach others how to do the same.

As has been stated previously, your mindset must change if you've been raised to think that life is all about living paycheck to paycheck if in fact you want to reach great heights of success and become totally free. Change is an inevitable constant, but choosing to change your internal mind and programming takes effort. It is deciding what type of changes will take place that determines where you'll end up.

This effort of being deliberate with the types of changes we make takes a great deal of faith. Ezra Taft Benson, the Secretary of Agriculture under President Eisenhower, said: "Every man eventually is backed up to the wall of faith, and there he must make his stand." In life, there comes a time when we all must "make [our] stand" so to speak. Identifying the course of action in line with our vision and goals is the first step. Once you have identified which action to take, it's time to be courageous and determined to see it through. By doing so, you will, in effect, "make [your] stand."

How to Train a Flea

The way to train a flea is an interesting one from which we can learn some valuable lessons. As a general rule, fleas can jump about as high as 13 inches. However, if you want to condition them to stay well below that number, it's quite simple. Place the fleas in a container with a lid on top. They will proceed to jump and jump even though they hit the top of the confined space. After some time, they will continue jumping but will no longer hit the top of the container. From then on, they will never jump higher than the height to which they were conditioned even after the lid is removed.

Humans are the same way; we begin life with so many hopes and dreams only to be ridiculed and censured to the point of discouragement. The opposition, hardships, and trials one faces too often leads to becoming like a trained flea— conditioned to the current environment in which one believes that something greater is always out of reach.

This does not have to be you. Remember what makes us humans different from every other living creature on this earth —our minds. Although certain trends, habits, and cultural customs begin conditioning us from birth, we have the ability to change even after years of this training. We must become aware of close mindedness at all possible occasions and use our mental faculties to open our minds toward possibility.

Think Outside the Box

Frequently we hear people say "think outside the box" or "I'm living in a box." When others refer to the box, they might as well be talking about the ordinary, the norm, or the comfort zone. It's a lot easier to stay in the comfort zone than to break out of it. We've all heard about or seen a little bird fight to hatch from an egg. It's always a dangerous and difficult excursion, but without it, they wouldn't have the strength to survive and continue to grow.

Many people live life inside their shell, so to speak, and rarely, if ever, break free or let alone crack the sides. They live in a box. In the movie *The Greatest Showman*, there's a scene where P.T. Barnum, the founder of the circus, is in pursuit of convincing Phillip Carlisle, a proper and traditionally wealthy man, to join him in the non-conventional development of the circus. In this scene, P.T. proudly declares this phrase to Phillip, "Comfort—The enemy of progress." How true that is! Think about it. When does the most growth occur in someone's life or what causes your muscles to get stronger? Tension, pressure, stress, and hardships often cause both physical and mental growth. That's why if the little birdie hatching from the egg receives help from an outside source to break free, it will die shortly after because it lacks the strength to keep living. Life is better outside the box. Break out of your shell and be who you're meant to be!

Rarely do we realize we're stuck in our own bubble until trying to escape it. Again, the factor is comfort. It's painful and often terrifying to leave our comfort zone and change our ways, but if we aren't improving, we're declining.

When you always do what you've always done, you'll always be where you've always been. That's insanity. Albert Einstein put it this way, "Insanity: [is the act of] doing the same thing over and over again and expecting different results." If this is true, and you're not getting the results you desire, then it may be time to make some changes.

Life is all about changing and becoming better than we were yesterday. This process doesn't happen overnight. It is for this reason that we ought to begin the process sooner than later.

Your responses to the questions posed at the end of Chapter 3 will be your guiding stars on your voyage through life.

In the Bible, Jesus Christ taught about the parable of a tree and its fruit. He teaches that a good tree produces good fruit, and an evil tree produces evil fruit—not the other way around. Jesus then gives the principle behind this analogy. "By their fruits ye shall know them."[2]

If you want apple juice, don't squeeze an orange. Nobody becomes extraordinary by doing the ordinary. This concept is simple. Your actions must be in line with your goals, or they'll always be just a cloud away.

College isn't a bad endeavor. There is great worth in an associates, bachelor's, master's, and doctorate degree. The decision to go to college is yours to make. If your goal is to become a doctor or a lawyer, you should get a degree. However, if your goal is to own or start a business from scratch, become a real estate agent or investor, actor, podcaster, YouTuber, plumber, or a number of various occupations, then college is not the only way. In fact, according to a study performed by TSheets published in 2021, only 9% of entrepreneurs have obtained a bachelor's degree in business.[3]

The founder of SpaceX and Tesla, Elon Musk, stated in an interview that "you can learn anything you want for free." He went on to say that colleges are for "fun and to prove you can do your chores, but they are not for learning." Those are some strong words from one of the richest men in the world. In the following chapters, we'll lay out certain skills and practices needed to achieve your goals. We'll also provide greater depth and insight on different venues to explore if you're not sure you want to be an employee the rest of your life.

---

1. Dispenza, Joe. (January, 2007). "Evolve Your Brain."
2. New Testament–Matthew 7:20 (KJV)
3. "39 Entrepreneur Statistics You Need to Know in 2021." Dragomir Simovic. August 2021. https://www.smallbizgenius.net/by-the-numbers/entrepreneur-statistics/

5

THE ART OF LEARNING

"Without moral and intellectual independence, there is no anchor for national independence."

-David Ben-Gurion

ART IS BEAUTIFUL. THERE ARE MANY TYPES OF ARTWORK, FROM Handel's Messiah to Michelangelo's Sistine Chapel and even to Jane Austen's classic novels. In all its many styles and forms, there is not a right or wrong way to portray oneself through the free expression of art. All forms are acceptable, and various individuals excel better with certain forms than others. There is no "one [form] fits all" in the world of art.

Learning is an art in and of itself. There is not one single method of learning. To the contrary, the various styles of learning are considerable in number, and like some artists are more talented in one form of art over another, some students learn faster with certain styles and methods of learning over others. Deciding which method to use is very much a case-by-case decision. What works best for one, may not be for another. Learning is optimal when it is personal and meaningful.

As discussed in Chapter 3, this is one of the primary reasons why the public school system isn't ideal for all students. Not only can your passionate flames of learning become extinguished by the required lectures and homework, but the method of learning employed caters to some and tends to be more difficult or even humiliating to others. Every student needs to learn at their own pace and in the way that suits them best. By teaching every student the same concept in the same way, not only does it become robotic, but it is like putting a square peg in a round hole. It won't work without severely damaging the peg. Like so, some students who would thrive under certain unpopular methods of teaching become severely damaged mentally and therefore physically due to the "one size fits all" mentality adopted all too often in the world of education.

To free ourselves from the shackles of constantly being told what to do, we need to demonstrate that we are capable of determining these things for ourselves. Remember, everything has a price, and freedom in learning is no different. We must become independent and self-reliant. This means taking charge of our own education. It means we realize we don't have all the answers but know where we can find them. There are tremendous advantages that come from being free to choose our style of learning and all it entails.

The Power to Choose

The primary benefit to taking charge of your learning experience is the freedom to choose the what, when, and how of your education. When attending a standard college or school, if that is the route you take, understand that you forfeit some control of certain classes and topics you'll study. You will have "general" education classes, as we have previously mentioned. If you are one who enjoys particular and specific guidance in certain tasks and educational goals, you will find this method highly effective. In contrast, there are many who for one reason or another, appreciate the opportunity to choose all of these things for themselves. Both include the power of choice, but one allows you to make a few choices and the other is a constant buffet approach to education.

The power to choose what, when, and how you study can be summed up in two words: intellectual freedom. It's the power to think for oneself, and as we heard previously, the only thing separating us from those in the animal kingdom is our mind. It would be safe to say then that if we aren't thinking for ourselves, we are no greater than a wild animal who lacks the ability to think.

As was heretofore mentioned, intellectual freedom has a price. If one desires to become an independent learner, they will need to train themselves with a different type of discipline than is learned in the most common approach to educating. The deadlines and structured assignments found in school hardly exist in the world of unconventionality. Obviously, whichever of the unconventional roads to education is taken, there will inevitably be forks along the way. However, you won't find a specific class by class, detailed structure to achieve true excellence. This must come from within.

Self-Starting Success

To become an independently educated person, you first must become a self-starter. Self-starters always rise to the top. They are the top 5%. They are the heavy hitters, the cream of the crop, and among the most independent. Being self-motivated is a prerequisite for creating and managing a business or an investment portfolio that is built to last.

If you work well under pressure or with a deadline, you'll most likely need to acquire the discipline to create these yourself. Establishing a vision and setting goals to reach it will provide the ideal structure for setting such deadlines. Although some are naturally blessed with these qualities, others must seek to develop them over time. If you're a born leader, you are a rare breed and ought to continue developing your natural abilities. However, if you don't find yourself with such qualities, don't fret. With consistent effort and practice, you can develop these attributes to the point that others might even mistake you for a naturally gifted leader. It is a worthy endeavor, and quite frankly, the world needs more of them. This reality could be yours. The underlying characteristic making it possible is passion.

You must be passionate about your vision and goals. Passion is the single most important aspect to success in studying independently. Your passion is your deepest desire. To maintain your excitement and enthusiasm for learning, you'll need to constantly be reaching for greater heights. We are meant to continually improve and become better. Identify what intrigues and excites you and pursue it. Fuel the fire!

Napoleon Hill is famous for associating two key principles in goal achievement. The inclusion of such prevents any obstacle from becoming insurmountable. The principles he emphasized are desire and faith. When desire is backed by faith, we can do anything. You've heard the cliché "where there's a will there's a way." Along the same vein but slightly more accurate would be the words of Napoleon Hill: "Desire backed by faith knows no such word as impossible."

In history, we find countless stories of impossible odds. We read so often of hefty opposition pitted against an idea led by one or many. Why is it that so often the idea or group facing impossible odds finds a way to come out on top? You guessed it, they back their deepest desire (passion) with the faith to achieve.

When we take time to scrutinize and study these stories in great depth, we typically find nothing exceptional about the people involved. In almost every aspect, they are what most would consider to be average. The distinguishing characteristic between these people and those who nobody cares to remember is the ability to do things in a certain way. This certain way is living life with passion, or in other words, allowing their deepest desires to be backed by the faith that they will come into fruition. So, if you feel average, you've already got what it takes to make history.

Independent Study Resources

In the world of open-minded education, you'll find innumerable resources for studying and learning. In all things, the source upon which you rely will greatly determine the results you experience. Be sure to follow and study the works and teachings given through a reliable source. In other words, make sure the people you listen to know what they're talking about. It's not possible to emphasize this point enough. In a world where anyone can say anything, great care must be taken to ensure the reliability of the information at hand. We've listed a few different study options below that we consider to be of great worth. This list is by no means inclusive and is meant to be added to on a regular basis.

Books/Audiobooks

One of your greatest resources is most likely sitting on the bookshelf in your home. Much has been said of reading and studying books. All self-starters read and encourage others to do the same. To fully develop the intellect, a person must have access to books and time to study them. Schedule time every day to invest in yourself and expand your knowledge through the study of great books. When putting together a plan of action to achieve your goals, daily reading is a must.

Audiobooks are an excellent way to be productive while in the car, cleaning the house, at the gym, or even in the shower. The libraries of audiobooks have been increasingly growing in recent years. Today, you will find nearly any book you can think of in audio form. When deciding whether to read the hard copy version of the book or listen to it, just be mindful of your learning style and the way in which you retain the most information. Some thrive with reading off the paper while others fall asleep. Some become invigorated when listening to audiobooks while others zone out. As in all things education, take time to determine what is right for you.

SEARCH ENGINES/ENCYCLOPEDIAS

We have all used these at one point or another. In fact, you probably used one today. This may have even been the mode in which you found this book. All in all, if you have a quick question or are seeking to dig a little deeper into a certain concept, search engines and encyclopedias (most of which are now digital) are an invaluable asset.

SEMINARS/WEBINARS

There's nothing like learning from the pros. In a seminar or webinar, you often get the best of everything in education. Generally, the presenter or speaker of the class is well educated and frequently an expert in the topic they are teaching, which presents a great opportunity for asking questions and learning how to model your actions after theirs for success. In addition to the speaker being a reliable source, you may have to pay to attend the seminar/webinar, which, as discussed previously in Chapter 3, naturally makes the attendee more dedicated to learning and applying what is taught.

YouTube

How many times have you wondered how to do something or how something works and turned to YouTube? Undoubtedly, many of us have found this to be yet another powerful resource. The value in knowing your way around YouTube is infinite. However, there's a time and place for it. Know when to use it and when to stay away from it. Seek to find those who are experienced and knowledgeable in the field on which they are filming.

Podcasts

A podcast is a beautiful thing. You can be listening to an expert anytime, anywhere, while doing practically anything. It's almost like you're there in the room with them. Just as some books edify, uplift, and educate, while others do not, podcasts can either help or hinder your progress. If listening to reliable, uplifting, and educating podcasts, these are practically in the same boat as an audiobook. Take some time to identify which podcasts help you achieve your goals, and hit the subscribe button.

Newsletters

Whether through email or the good old-fashioned mailers, regular newsletters can be great for staying on top of the latest trends in your realm of study. Carefully selected newsletters could be an excellent replacement for the hours of social media scrolling and wading through depressing news channels on TV just to stay informed. It's the perfect balance of staying informed and getting educated.

———

To summarize, these are but a few of the many resources at your disposal for conducting an in-depth study. You'll need to find what works best for you personally. It will take time and practice, especially if you're new to this whole educational responsibility thing. Be patient and persistent. As in all things, difficult times come and go. Remember, the most worthwhile endeavors in life take effort. The road to educate oneself is no exception. Don't get discouraged. It is in the most difficult moments that the lessons we learn are more powerful and profound than any other.

6

MENTORSHIPS—THE SPRINGBOARD FOR SUCCESS

"The delicate balance of mentoring someone is not creating them in your own image but giving them the opportunity to create themselves."

-Steven Spielberg

SINCE THE DAY YOU WERE BORN, YOU HAVE HAD A MENTOR, A teacher, a role model, someone whom you admired. This person set an example for you. You saw them succeed and wanted to share in that same success. Think of it. As a toddler, how did you first get the idea to start walking? Only after countless occasions of seeing others put one foot in front of the other did you conceive the idea.

People you admire influence your life not only by their actions but in the values by which they live. When you look up to someone, you scrutinize them, which not only leads to the study of their behavior, but the psychological processes of their mind. Their motives become your motives.

A mentor is one who has been where you are and has your overall success in their best interest. They do not expect money for the services they provide. The thrill of seeing you succeed is the only form of payment desired. Ulterior motives do not exist in a true mentor.

The best thing to do is to only take advice from those with whom you'd be willing to trade places. To disregard this principle is to put yourself in jeopardy of never living out your deepest dreams, which likely includes staying in bondage the entirety of your life. Be mindful of this principle.

When someone presents you with advice or counsel, consider the source. We recommend performing a simple evaluation to determine whether to follow the advice or to leave it be. First is to identify the lifestyle of the individual or group of individuals giving the advice. Second, remember the person you want to be and the type of life you want to live. If these are not coherent, throw out the advice and find another mentor. You wouldn't ask a dentist to paint your home. Similarly, you wouldn't ask a painter to fix your root canal. You can't give what you haven't got. Therefore, if those giving the advice haven't arrived there themselves, it's not worth your time.

Our lives are the compounded result of the way we live every single day. The consistent adherence to the counsel of a specific person or group will inevitably drive results that are shockingly similar to those from whom the advice originated. All we must do then to become great is to emulate the qualities and habits of those who have already achieved a goal of equal or greater magnitude than the one for which we're striving.

Listed below is a compilation of famous mentor and apprentice duos we have collected for your profit and learning. Notice that each of these duos were strikingly different yet similar in many other facets. Although we mix in a couple fictitious examples, the principles remain intact and applicable just the same. We highly encourage taking some time for an in-depth study of the qualities and traits in both the mentors and learners found in the list below. What made them a great mentor? How did the learner apply the advice given? How did they meet? What can you do to emulate or even replicate such a dynamic duo in your life?

Mentor	Learner
Steven Spielberg	J.J. Abrams
Steve Jobs	Mark Zuckerberg
Maya Angelou	Oprah Winfrey
Warren Buffett	Bill Gates
Stella Adler	Robert De Niro
Socrates	Plato
Gopal Krishna Gokale	Mahatma Gandhi
Mahatma Gandhi	Nelson Mandela
Professor Dumbledore	Harry Potter
Qui-Gon Jinn	Obi-Wan Kenobi

How do I select a mentor?

When seeking out a mentor, the question of selecting the right person is a common concern, and rightly so. From a mentor's perspective, there's nothing quite like coaching someone through a new or difficult situation and seeing your pupil succeed. It's a similar feeling to that of a parent who teaches their child to play a sport and watches them win a tournament, or the feeling of training someone in a skill you have worked hard and long to master and see your mentee succeed.

The single most important thing to look for in a mentor or coach is experience. Be certain to select a mentor who is doing what you want to do and has been where you are now. There are many fake people around you, so there may be some digging required on your part. Search out and find a mentor who is genuine and transparent. You should always be real and honest with everyone, but especially when in pursuit of a mentor. Don't force it! If the mentorship is going to be a win for both the mentor and the mentee (you), it'll need to be normal and natural.

Other things to keep in mind when seeking a mentor are their motives, ethics, and lifestyle. All of these are strongly associated, and it's essential to understand the difference between them. Depending on the person and situation, these may be easy or a bit more difficult to detect and evaluate.

MOTIVES

A motive is a reason for doing a certain task. Or, rather, your motive is the reason you get up every day. As discussed previously, your passion is your motive. If you can find your prospective mentor's passion and what makes them tick, then you've discovered and identified their motives.

ETHICS

The identification of one's ethics is not as cut and dry as determining their motives, but nonetheless, it is possible and has proven to be of great value in the selection of a mentor. Ethics are the moral principles and values that govern a person's behavior. To put it another way, your ethics are the way in which you go about working towards your goal. You can tell a lot about a person by their values and what they are willing to sacrifice for the achievement of their goals.

Let's consider the example of one who lives a healthy life. This consists of eating a variety of fruits, vegetables, and other nutritious foods. It also includes exercising regularly and getting adequate sleep. By considering this example in which one takes care of themselves by doing these activities, we may deduce the ethic or value of good health. One who lives a healthy lifestyle values their physical health so as not to place it on the altar of sacrifice for another goal. We may also infer the value of self-respect and confidence due to the efforts put forth in staying healthy. These are, however, assumptions based on one aspect of this person's life, but educated ones to say the least.

The only reason a person would sacrifice something they consider to be of value is in exchange for another aspect or ideal perceived to be of greater worth. Another name for this is priorities. Referring again to the healthy lifestyle example, if the value of health is important but valued slightly beneath that of family relationships and could only be achieved at the cost of damaging family ties, the moral of good health will not prevail. However, if ethics and values are of equal importance, the balance will be found and the demands of both may be appeased through what many would call a juggling act. This is why so many successful people stress the importance of living a balanced life.

LIFESTYLE

Both motives and ethics contribute to the type of lifestyle an individual attains and enjoys. Lifestyle is defined as the way in which one lives. If what a person focuses on grows, then one's lifestyle is a compounded result of the things they focus on. When we know their focus, we may, to an extent, learn some things about the ethics and motives beneath the surface. Ask yourself these questions: What is their family life like? What do they talk about? How do they dress? Are they financially sound? How do they spend their time? Do they have a social life? Are they happy? Would you enjoy living a similar lifestyle? Your answers to these questions will assist in determining if a particular person is a suitable mentor for you personally.

The Ideal Mentee

Just as you are determining which mentor would be right for you, mentors also carefully decide who their ideal mentees or learners would be. This brings up the questions, what is the ideal mentee and how can I be that person? The truth is, you can't force people to like you, but you can do certain things to make yourself more likeable as a learner and as a person in general. By doing so, you will effectively make it difficult for people not to like you. Here are three things you can do to increase your chances of finding the right mentor for you.

1. REMEMBER THAT YOU DON'T KNOW EVERYTHING.

Nobody likes to coach someone who thinks they know it all. You know what we mean. We've all met those people that think they're God's gift to mankind and everyone's knowledge is inferior to that of their own. Spoiler alert: you'll never know everything. The comforting fact is that it's not necessary. Remember, the reason to find a mentor is because you don't know everything. Isn't that a blessing? If you knew all there is to know about your area of focus, wouldn't that make life boring and dull? So, realize you don't know everything and enjoy being a beginner, at least for a little while.

2. ASK THE QUESTION EVEN IF YOU THINK YOU KNOW THE ANSWER.

There is no such thing as a stupid or useless question. If you're in a meeting either in a large group or a smaller setting, always have questions you can ask about your area of focus regardless of whether you know the answer or not. Simon Sinek uses the term "be the idiot." He uses this phrase because so many of us are afraid to ask questions because we fear we'll appear to others as being below the understanding and intelligence of those around us. However, what typically happens in these situations is the one who asks the question, or in other words, "the idiot," asks questions that coax answers and insight that many others in the group had questions about but lacked the courage to ask. When you ask these questions, you will not only learn more but will gain respect from those around you in addition to finding yourself in a more teachable position, which gives those with more experience (i.e., mentors) the chance to get to know you better, which may lead to a dynamic mentorship.

3. Treat everyone like they are the center of your universe.

Have you ever had someone listen to you? How did it feel? Speaking from personal experience, to have someone appreciate and acknowledge you to the point of truly listening is a feeling like no other. It is one of the most meaningful things you can do to build a relationship. Listening to someone is different than just nodding and saying "uh huh" or "that's cool." It involves much more. Listening is the art of making someone feel like the universe revolves around them. It involves being in the present moment, seeking to understand and making eye contact. If you want to learn more about these concepts, we highly recommend Dale Carnegie's book, *How to Win Friends and Influence People.* It is an indispensable resource in this regard. More on this later.

Where do I find a mentor?

There are suitable mentors with experience in your desired field of study and labor everywhere. In fact, with social media and the recent advances in technology, you can connect with people in any part of the world at any time of day. Regarding a specific location where you can find these people, this varies depending on where you live in the world, but there are a few universal places you may find and acquire a mentor.

The first and quite possibly the easiest place to find a coach is on a jobsite. Depending on the field in which you desire to enter, getting a job and learning from a professional could be the best option. When looking for work, always, always look for skills and abilities you can learn from the job instead of just looking at the dollar sign. When your primary goal is to learn from your work and not just to earn, it becomes much easier to get a job, and most often, you will end up getting paid much more than anyone else in the field simply due to your thirst for knowledge and experience. In short, a great place to find a mentor is a job in which your primary goal is to work for education and experience.

Most universities require that you intern with a company in your field of study to obtain real world experience. These internships are a great opportunity to meet experts and learn skills and aspects of a job that the classroom cannot offer. An internship is a valuable resource. If you have the chance to intern, take it. If you don't have such an option, a job in which the primary focus is to learn and network will give you a similar experience.

The final place we wanted to bring to your attention isn't what you'd expect. Actually, it's not considered a place at all. Most people overlook it when searching for a mentor because it's been around for over a thousand years. This place can be described in a word—books. Books can be a great mentor. Or rather, you can get to know a mentor by reading their writings compiled into a book. The teachings and insights found in published materials can be personal and life changing. It is a different way of looking at the concept of mentoring, but it is still a valid and essential facet to receive needed instruction. It's the perfect blend of independent study and mentorship all in one place.

Mentor versus Consultant

Now that we know the essence of how to select and where to find a mentor, it's time to clarify the difference between a mentor and a consultant. A mentor is not a consultant, although you may consult with your mentor on certain issues for guidance and counsel. They are in fact quite different while at the same time remarkably similar. Let's break it down and see what differentiates the two.

A consultant is a professional with a considerable amount of expertise in the field in which you are seeking assistance. They know their stuff and rightfully so. They have been through the experiences and know their way in and out of their specialized field. The advice and counsel given from a consultant ought to be followed with as much adherence as would be that of a mentor.

The cardinal difference between a mentor and a consultant is the expectation of pay. As we mentioned, a real mentor doesn't expect to receive any monetary compensation for coaching and guiding while a consultant expects to be paid for their services. This does not discredit or downplay the advice or assistance both a mentor and a consultant provide, just a noteworthy difference in your pursuit of finding a more experienced soul to lead and guide you on your journey.

One of my greatest mentors I've been blessed to have in my life is my father. He's been there since day one through thick and thin. There is no expectation of money or other source of compensation for his efforts. He listens, advises, recommends, and coaches. By no means would I consider him to be a perfect mentor for everyone. However, by divine design, he is the perfect coach and mentor for me.

Regardless of whether you have a father- or mother-like figure, we guarantee you have people in your life you admire for who they are. You see them as an example worthy of emulating. If you haven't identified one such individual in your life, look around and open your eyes. It may be a family friend, grandparent, sibling, or someone you haven't met yet. If they are sought out, they will be found.

You will find a notable difference between striving for success with a mentor on your side versus without such a luxury. There is no replacement for a good mentor who coaches, trains, and challenges you to become better than you were yesterday. If you take advantage of the advice and insight given in this chapter, you will be on your way to identifying the right mentor for you and becoming the person everyone would be honored to teach and coach.

We again encourage you to review the list of mentors and learners given in this chapter and ask yourself these questions as you study: What made these mentors so great? How did the learner and the mentor meet? What can I do to find mentors like these? Remember to not take advice from people who aren't successful or who don't have experience in your area of study or work. Unless they have had the experience for which you yearn, their words are hollow. That being said, if you seek for an outstanding mentor, you will find one.

PART III

CHANGING THINGS UP

7

EXPLORING ALL OPTIONS

"People will always try to stop you from doing the right thing if it is unconventional."

-Warren Buffet

Do Something Unconventional

UNCONVENTIONALITY CAN SOMETIMES BE THE BETTER WAY. After all, who dictates what is unconventional? What Henry Ford and Thomas Edison did was considered unconventional at the time because they both chose to stand out in the crowd and create something revolutionary. Let's examine what specifically these men did that was unconventional.

For Henry Ford, we will be specifically addressing his journey in producing the 8-cylinder motor. As many people may know, Mr. Ford wanted to create an engine that had the entire eight-cylinders cast in a single block. After proposing the idea to his engineers, they retorted that it was impossible. However, despite their disbelief, Mr. Ford managed to get the engine made thanks to his relentless and unwavering encouragement and patience with the engineers. This engine naturally had more horsepower, which allowed larger vehicles to be manufactured for the benefit of the world.

Similarly, Thomas Edison was unconventional when he invented a variety of items, most notably the electric light bulb. This technology changed the world's perspective of electricity on an astronomical level and is still widely used today. When he boldly announced that he was going to invent an electric light that would illuminate the world and replace gaslights, there were many scientists and critics that claimed such a feat was impossible. In the end, Edison succeeded and produced the world's first electric light bulb despite the harsh opposition.

What did these men have in common? Most notable was the fact that they both received very little "formal" education. They were, nonetheless, highly educated individuals. Edison received virtually all his education from his mother. On the other hand, Ford received a more formal education. Yet, he was far too fascinated with engineering to bother with much more education in the classroom after the age of 16.

Now, as we learned in the first chapter, the education system has changed—and not exactly for the better—since these men were of that age. In addition, these examples are not to discredit what you can learn through "formal education." Rather, we are merely trying to demonstrate and help you realize that if college is not for you, there are other ways you can achieve your goals.

While Thomas Edison and Henry Ford experienced great success in the course of their lifetimes, they also endured heavy opposition. We feel it essential that you learn how to deal with such opposition. That's why we will talk more about how you can handle the critics and opposition you will inevitably face in a later chapter.

What are the trades?

Contrary to what many people think, the trades are both profitable and worthy careers for anyone. The standard mindset toward education promotes going to college, getting a job, retiring at age 65, etc. There isn't much talk of alternative paths such as the trades, owning a business, or pursuing other opportunities that don't require traditional curriculums.

There are many different trade opportunities available. Here is a short list of some of the more well-known trade careers available to you today. When you look at this list, we want you to think about how important each of these professions are in a functioning community.

CARPENTER

A carpenter specializes in crafting with wood. They do the brunt work of building new houses, and they can also perform smaller wood jobs like cabinets, furniture, and trims.

PLUMBER

Plumbers are professionals at anything related to running water. Some of the jobs they perform can be as simple as fixing water leaks and as advanced as collaborating with an architect for new construction.

LANDSCAPER

Landscaping is a broader profession than many of these other trades listed. Landscapers can specialize in yard maintenance like mowing lawns and trimming trees, or they can focus on the larger scale jobs that include designing and transforming a yard to a client's liking. Many landscapers will perform all of the above.

Electrician

An electrician's primary job consists of maintaining and installing wiring for buildings, troubleshooting and fixing wiring, and even working with outdoor telephone/power lines. They also work with an architect for the construction of new homes.

Painter

Painters are experts at painting all kinds of products. A painter knows how to clean, sand, prime, and paint cars, buildings, etc. An experienced painter can paint interiors and exteriors of buildings. They work with both general contractors and individual residents.

HVAC Technician

HVAC (heating, ventilation, and air conditioning) technicians are professionals at maintaining, repairing, and installing equipment to heat and cool your home or workspace. Some technicians can specialize in sales and service while others specialize in installation or a combination of these.

Auto Mechanic

Mechanics troubleshoot, maintain, and repair road vehicles. An experienced mechanic should know the ins and outs of a functioning vehicle. Many auto mechanics start as apprentices and work their way up to becoming masters in their trade.

LOCKSMITH

As if it were not obvious, locksmiths specialize in repairing, installing, and other services pertaining to anything that locks. This includes homes, cars, offices, and safes. If you lock yourself out of your house, this is the person you should call to come to your rescue.

EXTERMINATOR/PEST CONTROL

Nobody wants pests and rodents running around inside their house. This is why we have exterminators and pest control professionals. These tradespeople are trained to know how and where to catch and trap all kinds of rodents and pests.

Why the trades?

The trades can give you a jump start on your career by either starting as an apprentice or attending the one-to-two-year trade school instead of spending four years for a bachelor's degree. Despite what some individuals will try to tell you, you can still make good money in careers that don't require a full four years of education. In many, if not all of the trades, you can work your way up to earn six figures annually.

Now, we want you to look at each of these trades we listed above. You've probably benefited from them at one point in your life. One thing they have in common is the fact that these, as well as others, are crucial for a functioning society. The trades are literally the foundation to all countries, cities, and homes. If we didn't have people working the trades, all of us would practically be living in a third-world country.

If what was mentioned above wasn't enough, there are additional benefits to entering the trades. Let's go over some additional reasons why the trades are worth looking into, as well as what makes them so important. Our hope is that after you finish reading this chapter, you'll see the value in pursuing a trade and, in turn, have a greater appreciation for these careers.

Listed below are three advantages that come with entering the trade workforce. These perks begin before your first day on the job. We point out that the methods of teaching used in vocational and specialized schools are both effective and impressive. It's also comforting to realize there's a great deal of job security in the trades. They're not going to be obsolete any time soon. The last benefit we describe is the long, lost concept of daily face-to-face personal interaction. These are just a few, but let's look at what makes these possible.

1. IMPROVED LEARNING EXPERIENCE IN TRADE SCHOOLS

Trade and vocational schools are specialized and focused. This is the reason why it only takes about two years to graduate. They focus on what is needed to effectively and efficiently achieve the desired outcome and leave behind the non-essential material. In other words, they omit the general education courses required at most colleges and allow students to hone in to obtain specialized knowledge.

The learning experience in the majority of trade schools is often a cut above other educational institutions for a number of reasons. This is due to the difference in class structure and content used at these schools. The classes are typically structured to be smaller than many traditional college classes, which allows for a more individual focused learning experience. They're also structured to have more hands-on practice, granting students the ability to accelerate the rate of retention and application for the various tasks they'll perform once they enter the field. We say this because by combining auditory, visual, and tactile learning styles to a class, the students reap a longer lasting learning experience and understanding than if only one or two methods are employed. We touched on this briefly in Chapter 3.

There is a minimal amount of formal education required to obtain a job in the trades. Did you know that you can get the same job in the trades without a degree as someone with a degree? This is true because many companies hire individuals with little to no education or experience on the job. While you would naturally start with a lower pay, that does not mean you are not able to work your way up to be an expert. What matters more than your education is your work ethic. As discussed in Chapter 6, strive to be the ideal mentee. Anything you learn at a trade school you can be taught on the job. However, this is not to say trade schools should not be utilized. Whether you choose to attend a trade school or learn on the jobsite is a personal preference, as there are advantages to both. Do what works best for you!

Because trade school typically only takes one to two years to complete, there comes the reduced cost of both money and time. We have already discussed in an earlier chapter the fact that so many students continue to pay their student loans long after graduation. With one to two years instead of the usual three to four years, you're able to avoid getting into such massive debt.

2. Business/Job Security

Trade schools offer skills that stand the test of time. Another great benefit of a trade school is that most of what you learn will not be phased out over the years. For example, in 50 years, everyone is still going to want to style their hair, need electrical work done, and build a home. Again, the point is, the trades have and, for the foreseeable future, will continue to thrive because of their significance in everyone's lives.

The men and women of the trades provide indispensable and life-sustaining services. Can you imagine living in a place that gets over 100, let alone 90 degrees, without any air conditioning? And what about living in a place where you don't have any running water? You can easily come up with an example for each and every trade because we utilize their fruits every single day.

There are opportunities everywhere. According to the Air Conditioning Contractors of America (ACCA), the HVAC market alone is projected to increase in value from $25.6 billion to $35.8 billion by 2030, and HVAC jobs are projected to increase by 13% from 2018 to 2028.[1] And since we are talking about the HVAC market, did you know there are over 100 thousand HVAC companies in the U.S.? And that number is only growing. As more and more people spread out and cities grow, the demand for HVAC, as well as the other trades, will only rise.

HOW THE TRADES WERE AFFECTED BY THE 2020 COVID-19 PANDEMIC

One of the most world-changing events of 2020 was the Covid-19 pandemic. In March 2020, businesses were forced to shut down for a time as a way to slow the infection rate. By now, you may be one of the many that are groaning because of the fact we're talking about Covid-19, as most of us have grown tired of hearing about it in one way or another.

So, what does the pandemic have to do with the trades? In many ways the trades didn't only survive the pandemic, they thrived in the pandemic. During the lockdowns, many businesses were forced to shut their doors for a while as all except the "essential" businesses were shut down in many areas. The "essential" businesses included most food services, virtually all the trades, and some others that were allowed to remain open at the time. While the "non-essential" businesses were closed, industries like the trades boomed as they were able to continue to do business with some obvious safety precautions.

Prior to the pandemic, many people were already working from home, however, Covid-19 accelerated this number exponentially. With this being the case, the demand for heating, cooling, plumbing, and electrical work in each home increased greatly. Faster, better, and more affordable service was requested. After some adjustment, these needs are being met. Technicians and workers continue to labor and help customers stay comfortable, healthy, and safe in their homes today.

This is not to say that the trades didn't struggle during the pandemic. In fact, within months, many businesses had problems getting the materials needed to perform their work. The slowed import of parts and materials provided plenty of challenges. Even over a year after the initial lockdowns, some of these businesses still struggle to get a hold of their materials. Despite these new challenges, many businesses have been able to not only find a way to survive the pandemic but to thrive in it.

3. DAILY FACE-TO-FACE INTERACTION

You interact with customers more in the trades than in many other jobs. With more and more jobs becoming virtual and distant, the trades can provide you with the opportunity to get out in the field and interact with people. It is safe to say that most people appreciate face-to-face interaction as part of their job. According to a 2009 Forbes Insights survey, 84% of the 750+ surveyed business executives expressed that they preferred face-to face meetings over virtual platforms.[2] Because most jobs in the trades provide face-to-face interaction with customers, you're able to build strong relationships between the company and the customer. This often results in a greater experience for both the customer and the person providing the service.

Other Opportunities

Now that we've gone over the trades and talked about some of the different aspects of those industries, let's talk about some other paths you ought to consider when searching for a career that best suits you. The careers listed below are some other suitable options for anyone who wants to consider all their options. There are many other options not listed below, but we hope this list gives you a taste of some of the many opportunities available and gets you excited about the vast number of possibilities that exist for you. While we provide a brief description of each of these careers as well as some of the education required, we cannot stress enough the value that comes from doing your own research. We highly encourage you to find out for yourself the specifics of any path you consider.

POLICE FORCE

If you're interested in becoming a part of the force that keeps neighborhoods and communities safe and orderly, then the police force might be for you. The only formal education required to become a police officer is a high school diploma. Of course, after high school, you must complete a widespread and specialized training that's provided at the police academies on the local, regional, or state levels.

FIREFIGHTER

A firefighter's main job focuses not only on putting out fires but first to save the lives in danger in the event of a fire or other disaster. To become a firefighter, you need to have at least a high school diploma. However, if you become an EMT and/or earn a degree in fire science, it will improve your chances of being hired and potentially impact how fast you move up the ranks. You can still get a job and move up the ranks without any additional education though.

EMT

An EMT (Emergency Medical Technician) must complete a CPR certification, an emergency medical technology program (which usually takes one to two years), as well as pass a certification exam. An EMT can be a great option if you are passionate about helping people medically but don't want to get a college degree.

DENTAL ASSISTANT

If you want to pursue a career working in a dentist's office but would rather start working sooner than later, a dental assistant career is a great doorway to get there. A dental assistant's job varies from performing x-rays to helping the dentist fill a cavity. The majority of states require you to become a certified dental assistant through programs qualified by the Commission on Dental Accreditation. There are some states that currently do not require you to get any certification to become a dental assistant, however, it may be a good option to complete the certification to have better chances at a job, especially if job opportunities are low in your area. You may also need to have CPR training, so be sure to check your local requirements for what is needed for you to become a dental assistant.

MEDICAL ASSISTANT

Medical assistants, or clinical assistants, have the primary responsibility of scheduling appointments, taking care of insurance billing, and handling medical records. Depending on the state, the company, and your experience/qualifications, you could also find yourself working more with patients directly. The only education required to become a medical assistant is a high school diploma. All other training is acquired on the job. However, there are various optional certifications that you may obtain that will improve your resume.

VETERINARY TECHNICIAN

If you enjoy spending time with animals and would like to make a career out of caring for them, then this is a viable option. Veterinary technicians spend most of their time performing tasks like taking x-rays, administering vaccines, as well as various laboratory work. One may become a veterinary technician with two years of education through an AVMA approved program supplemented with adequate hands-on training.

COSMETOLOGIST

For those interested in a career in cosmetology, a cosmetologist can be a great option for you. To become certified as a cosmetologist, you will need to complete courses at a state licensed cosmetology school that usually take 9 to 18 months, depending on the program you choose. You may then need to spend a certain amount of time training or as an intern. Finally, you receive your certification upon complying with all the requirements and passing the state licensing exam.

The Power of Apprenticeship

Before we address apprenticeships again, we would like to first specify what kind of apprenticeship of which we are speaking. Throughout this book, when we discuss apprentices and mentors, we are talking about those of private parties and individuals. In other words, we are not addressing registered apprenticeship programs that are made possible through the government. We are simply speaking of the basic principles of apprenticeship. We do not recommend whether or not you pursue one of these programs, as that is up to you and what you feel works best.

If attending a postsecondary school is not your forte, then you may want to consider an apprenticeship. As mentioned in Chapter 6, through an apprenticeship, you will have the opportunity to learn and improve your skills through your mentor. There are many advantages to pursuing an apprenticeship in the trades or the many other occupations that apprenticeships are offered.

We hope this chapter got you thinking about various options and opportunities that most often aren't even considered. There are both upsides and downsides to all of these various career paths. When all is said and done, it all goes back to what your personal goals and passions are. It is crucial that you choose something that brings happiness and gives you a sense of purpose and fulfillment. We continue to bring this point up and even expound upon it more in a later chapter. For now, consider and ponder on what **your** passion is and what gives **you** a sense of fulfillment.

---

1. Air Conditioning Contractors of America (ACCA). "The HVAC Industry Is Heating Up." https://www.acca.org/hvac-industry-growth
2. "Business Meetings-The Case for Face-to-Face." Forbes Insights. https://www.forbes.com/forbesinsights/Business_Meetings_FaceToFace/

SUPPLEMENTATION WITH INVESTMENTS

"The biggest risk of all is not taking one."

-Mellody Hobson

ARE YOU AN INVESTOR? HAVE YOU EVER THOUGHT ABOUT becoming one? We're all taught how to work for money, but did you know you can have your money work for you? That very well may be a worthy definition of investing. For most people, when they hear the word "investment," they think of the stock market and/or their 401(k) plan. While these can be profitable investments, they are extremely volatile, and the value of such tends to fluctuate on a regular basis for a number of reasons. There are many better options where you can invest your money either for retirement, supplemental income, or even to become financially free.

The reason the rich invest their money is because they know that the two ways to earn money are through working for a paycheck or investing in assets (things that are producing positive cash flow) whose value will increase over time. Millionaires know that directly working for their money via a regular paycheck is not the most effective way to generate generational wealth. That is why they invest in assets like real estate and businesses, therefore providing multiple streams of income. Instead of spending their time working for a paycheck, they spend their time working for knowledge to reduce the risk of each investment, and as a result of their applied knowledge, increase their wealth.

This chapter is designed to give you an overview of the concept of investing, as well as some of the different ways you can invest. The world of investing is both exciting and complex, which is why it is impossible to teach you everything there is to know about investing in a single chapter. We highly recommend you continue your education on investing beyond this book and throughout your life.

The Basics of Investing

If you are looking for a way to "get rich quick," this is not the place. Investing, most often, takes time and patience to build a large sum of money or riches. Now, everyone's situation is different; some people take longer than others, but what matters most is you are improving and progressing daily.

The concept of investing money is not complicated. In simplest terms, the act of investing is when you allocate a certain amount of money for a time with the expectation or hope of a return or profit. That's it. So, if it's that simple, why don't more people do it? Well, to become a savvy investor, one must know the ins and outs of what they are getting themselves into. Even if you have learned everything there is to know about investing, there is always the possibility you will lose money. That is why we recommend you learn as much as you can before placing your money into any investment so as to minimize the amount of risk you'll be taking.

In the financial world, there's a saying that goes, "The higher the risk, the higher the return." Think about that for a moment. Now, for some investments, this may ring true, but it shouldn't be taken as the gospel truth. Let's use an analogy to prove this point.

Have you ever trusted someone to fix an appliance or piece of equipment of which you had very little knowledge? What gave you comfort in relying on them to fix it? Was it a gamble or an educated guess? There have been one too many companies or one-man-band shops who claim they know how to fix something and end up butchering it even more than if they hadn't touched it to begin with. How do you avoid this? Invest some time and maybe even some money in yourself. Acquire some knowledge. You don't have to go overboard and become someone who fits under the mantra "jack of all trades expert of none," but you would do well to become well rounded in the knowledge that makes a difference.

We've all had an experience in which we needed to trust someone else to do something we couldn't do for ourselves due to a lack of knowledge and experience. We've also all experienced betrayal or improper placement of our trust. In light of this, we learned that not all knowledge is created equal. Some people who claim to be experts are beginners. This is true even for the financial world.

Just because someone has a license to touch your money doesn't mean they know what's best for you and your goals. The best way to minimize the risk of any investment, whether through a financial planner, close friend, complete stranger, or your own independent endeavors, is knowledge. Gather as much knowledge as you can in the field of money and investing for the realization of your goals. It is sometimes true that "the higher the risk, the greater the return," but a slightly more accurate saying could be, "The higher the risk, the [lesser the education.]" Don't let that be you! It's not worth the risk. Get smart!

> *"Wisdom is not a product of schooling but of the lifelong attempt to acquire it."*
>
> *-Albert Einstein*

Some of the best material for learning about these topics comes from the books that investing professionals write and endorse. Many of these books contain experiences of writers including mistakes and failures, which provide the great lessons on how you can become a savvy investor. As we mentioned in the chapter on the art of learning, studying these nuggets of wisdom from those with more experience can almost be compared to being mentored on a personal level.

> *"The more you read, the more things you will know. The more you learn, the more places you will go."*
>
> *-Dr. Seuss*

This principle of learning applies to all investments you decide to pursue. The less you know about something, or in this case an investment, the more likely you are to lose money. As John F. Kennedy once said, "The greater our knowledge increases, the more our ignorance unfolds."

The Effects of Inflation

"Savers are losers." -Robert T. Kiyosaki

Why not just save your cash instead of taking risks on investments? Most people will save money for their future, education, or retirement in the form of cash. People have money in emergency funds they save for hard times, vacation funds, and often for a new car or house. Money in and of itself holds no value but is a mode of exchange. These are all worthy reasons to save your money, however, the fact of the matter is that saving money is losing money. Yes, you read that sentence correctly. When you save money, you're losing it. The amount of green stuff you have remains the same, but the buying power decreases as the federal reserve continues to print it. This is Economics 101. When the supply of something increases, the demand typically decreases, and therefore the value of the item drops.

Back in 1944, the United States and a number of other countries made an agreement to tie their currencies to the value of gold, therefore fixing the amount each U.S. dollar was worth. This event is known as the Bretton Woods agreement. As you may know, there is a limited supply of gold on the earth, which limits the supply of currency that could be created under this arrangement. With the U.S. dollar backed by gold, saving was a worthy endeavor because the value of the dollar was fixed, or in other words, the dollar wouldn't lose purchasing power.

So what happened? If we fast forward to 1971, we find the answer. This was the year President Richard Nixon took the United States off the gold standard by bringing the Bretton Woods agreement to an end, thereby turning the U.S. dollar into a fiat currency. In terms of currency, the term "fiat" means to have no intrinsic value or any use value. Nixon's actions pushed the nation into an inflationary period.

To inflate is to enlarge. When we speak of inflation from an economic standpoint, we mean to enlarge or expand the supply of money. One of the key indicators for inflation is a consistent increase in prices, which therefore leads to the need for higher wages to compensate for such an increase in the cost of living. This was made possible by the one and only President Nixon.

The primary cause of inflation is the expansion of the supply of money by the federal reserve. And again, because the dollar is no longer backed by something of actual value (i.e., gold), the government can essentially pull dollars out of their backside. Wow! Maybe mom and dad were wrong. Maybe money really does grow on trees—that is, if you're the federal reserve.

If we look at the present-day circumstances, we see many rapid changes seemingly on a daily basis. Whether the cause is a pandemic, civil unrest, political conflicts, or another matter, anyone who is economically informed and up-to-date on current events cannot deny the accelerated rate of inflation we have seen in great part due to the massive sum of money the federal reserve pumps into the economy through handouts and both forgivable and non-forgivable loans. The intentions may be pure, but once you start down the slippery slope of inflation, there's no turning back.

Let's look at the 12-month period of April 2020 to April 2021. As of April 2021, the 12-month inflation rate was over 3%. This means that if you bought a gallon of milk in April 2020 priced at $3, the same gallon of milk a year later would cost about $3.10. Inflation decreases the value of dollars. Wouldn't you rather turn your long-term savings into something with lasting value than slowly watch it sink into a worthless stash of cash?

For another example, let's say you save $1,000 cash in a locked safe inside your home for emergencies in April of the year 2017. At this time, the retail gasoline price per gallon is about $2.52. Of course, if you were to live in a place with a larger economy like California, you would likely be paying well over $4 in many areas. As time passes and the government continues to print money, you still manage to keep that same $1,000, but in April 2021, a gallon of gasoline now costs you approximately $2.94 per gallon. That's a price increase of over 16%. In order to offset the effects of the inflation, you would need about $1,090 in your safe instead of only $1,000. If the price of gasoline goes up, it's safe to assume the price of all goods will soon follow, because oil is used for so many things and in so many places from asphalt to rubber and even plastics. That is why we recommend that you invest in something that has lasting value.

How can you save your riches?

Now that we know the basics behind the act of President Nixon, we understand that saving your money in the form of cash isn't the best way to preserve your riches from generation to generation. The best way to stay safe in the storms and waves of inflation is to find an item that will maintain its value indefinitely and independent of any governmental organization. For thousands of years, gold, silver, and a number of other precious metals have been used to measure the riches and net worth of families and leaders around the world. If you're looking for a hedge against inflation, these metals may be a worthy investment.

To illustrate that these metals maintain the same value and the effects of inflation on such, we have pulled some statistics to make it more real for all of us. Based on such stats, we learn that $1 in 2010 is equal to $1.22 in 2021. In other words, the U.S. dollar has inflated by roughly 22% since 2010. On the other hand, the dollar value of gold has increased by at least 40% in the same time period. Thus, we see that gold and other precious metals hold their value through inflation. You won't get rich by investing in these metals, but you will ensure the preservation of your riches and hard work. To reiterate, just because gold, silver, or another precious metal costs more U.S. dollars does not mean it goes up in value. The only value that changes is that of the fiat currency (i.e., the dollar), and this is only due to the influx of U.S. dollars in circulation.

The Magic of Compound Interest

Whether investing or borrowing money, there are many ways interest comes into play. When you apply for a loan to buy a car or house, you agree to pay back the principal amount, generally in monthly payments, plus an interest percentage. Another way interest comes into play is through various retirement and savings plans in which you contribute a certain amount of money that grows over time through this phenomenon we call interest. We'll talk more about these retirement plans later in this chapter, but for now just know that there are two main ways interest can be expressed. These are known as simple and compound.

Simple interest is usually expressed in a fixed rate through the entirety of an agreed period of time. An example of this is a car loan. When you apply for a car loan, you are charged an interest rate based on the regulations set by the lender and your credit score. You are then required to make payments on the principal amount of the loan plus the interest.

To simplify, let's say you apply for a five-year (60 month) car loan of $10,000. You agree to the fixed interest rate of 5% and sign the papers. This means you will be paying about $198 a month for five years (assuming that you don't make any additional principal payments). After the five years pass, you will have paid the principal of $10,000 plus roughly $1,100 in interest payments for a grand total of $11,100. Keep in mind, this example is oversimplified to teach the principle of simple interest. You may be wondering why we said 5% and came up with $1,100 in interest. There are many variables that come into play when getting a car loan. We also do not consider ourselves professionals when it comes to calculating car loans, so please see professionals if you find yourself pursuing one. If you must take out a loan to purchase a car, do so prudently.

Compound interest, unlike simple interest, accumulates over a period of time. It's all about exponential growth. To illustrate this concept, if you were to open a retirement account with compound interest and initially invested $10,000 and contributed $500 monthly for 30 years at an interest rate of 10%, you would end up with a grand total of $1,161,458.16. That's pretty impressive. Of course, over the 30 years you've contributed $190,000, but now it's well over $1 million. If you would have saved the money under your mattress instead, you would still have the same old $190,000. See Figure 2 below for a better picture of just how much exponential growth we're looking at. Compound interest is the type of interest most sought after when investing because of this snowball effect. It starts out small but grows to an astonishingly high amount with time and patience.

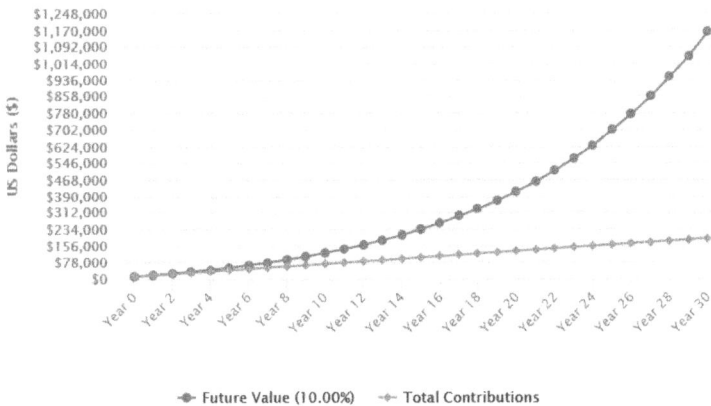

(Figure 2)

Albert Einstein is famous for terming compound interest as the eighth wonder of the world, but the best part of that quote is the phrase that follows. It reads, "He who understands it, earns it. He who doesn't, pays it." You don't want to be caught on the paying side of this type of interest! You'll go broke as fast as you can say, "I wish I learned how to use this in school!"

To summarize, simple interest is the most advantageous when you are paying, but compound interest should be your priority if you're trying to get paid (usually through an investment). If it was not obvious enough, you want to avoid any situation where you're paying compound interest like the plague. In any investment, whether the interest is simple or compound, you'll want to ensure that your return on investment outpaces the rate of inflation. This is how the top dogs evaluate and manage their money.

The Stock Market

When you tell anyone you're an investor, their mind almost immediately goes to the stock market. Even though it is the most popular form of investing, many people who invest in the stock market are either gamblers, bandwagoners, or just losing boat loads of money. There are many different ways to invest in the stock market. The key is to find the most profitable investing strategies and use them to make a whole lot more money and legally pay less taxes to put more moolah in your pocket. All in all, you can make a pretty penny investing in the stock market if you're smart and know what you're doing.

In this section, we'll give a brief description of various ways to invest in the stock market. After reading through the many methods listed below, if any catches your attention, we highly recommend performing extensive research before dropping money on the investment. Remember, the best way to lessen your risk is to gain as much knowledge as possible before making a move.

BUYING AND SELLING SHARES

A stock is a security that represents the ownership of a part or share of a corresponding corporation. This in turn will enable you to have a portion of the corporation's profits based on how many shares owned. You can buy and sell stock shares on various stock exchange platforms.

BONDS

A bond is a unit of corporate debt issued by a company and is securitized into tradable form. In other words, a bond is issued when an investor lends money to a company or other entity with an agreement to pay the loan back with interest in payments over the course of a predetermined amount of time. The interest for these payments can be either fixed or variable depending on the agreement that is made when the bond is created. Bonds are usually used by many forms of government and corporations to borrow and raise capital for the various expenses and projects they encounter. These can be purchased and traded publicly or privately.

MUTUAL FUNDS

A mutual fund is a pool of investor's money, which typically consists of a combination of securities such as stocks and bonds. These funds are managed by financial planners and professionals. One advantage to mutual funds is they allow small investors to enter into professionally managed portfolios at a lower upfront cost. A common way you earn money in these funds is through distributions from stocks and bonds. You can also earn capital gains through a mutual fund if the fund has sold securities whose value has increased. However, these funds charge fees and commissions, so keep that in mind when considering investing. Because mutual funds are managed by a fund manager who is hired by a board of directors, as an investor, you have little control of how the money in the fund is managed or in what they invest.

ETFs

An ETF, or exchange traded fund, is a security that usually follows an index like the S&P 500 and is created by a provider who owns the original assets that consist completely of a combination of stocks, bonds, and commodities. The provider uses the fund to track the performance of the assets and then sells shares to investors. The shareholders can then earn dividends on the fund. You can buy and sell ETFs through online brokers and broker dealers.

STOCK OPTIONS

A stock option gives an investor the right to buy or sell a stock at a price and on a date that is predetermined in the agreement. In other words, by using stock options, you can buy stocks speculating that the stock will rise or fall and then sell the stocks at a specific date that both parties agree upon. The two types of options are puts and calls. If you choose a put option, you are betting that a stock's value will fall. Conversely, with a call option, you are speculating that a stock's value will rise. Options yield high returns but can be very risky ways to invest in the stock market, so invest wisely and learn plentifully.

Universal Life (UL) and Indexed Universal Life Insurances (IUL)

A UL insurance, or Universal Life insurance, is a permanent life insurance that has an investment savings element with small premiums. These policies are similar to term life insurance with either flexible, single, or fixed premiums (it will depend on the company and policy). They will provide you with a death benefit as well.

An IUL, or Indexed Universal Life insurance policy, is similar to a UL but allows you to use either a fixed or an equity index account. These policies are less risky than ULs because none of your money is invested in an equity position. One advantage of an IUL policy is it offers tax-deferred accumulation of cash for your retirement while still maintaining a death benefit. They are often nicknamed the "rich man's Roth" because you can select a plan with no limit to how much cash you can pour into it during the course of a year depending how the plan is structured. These life insurance policies must be structured a certain way to truly maximize their benefit to help you achieve your goals, so be sure to find a broker who knows your goals and has the experience necessary to set the plan up accordingly.

Depending on the plan you select and how many years you contribute to these life insurance plans, you need not fear of running out of money before you give up the ghost. Many, if not all, of these plans use compound interest, so your balance just keeps growing exponentially year after year. In addition to exponential growth while you're living, these plans also blossom when you die. So, if your goal is to create generational wealth (i.e., a family bank, as mentioned by Douglas Andrew in his book *Entitlement Abolition*), you would do well to take a deeper dive in learning more about these specific plans. It's never too early to start!

401(k) AND IRA RETIREMENT PLANS

Many people have the opportunity to participate in an employer sponsored 401(k) or choose to prepare for retirement independently with an Individual Retirement Plan (IRA). These plans provide employees with relatively simple ways to save for their retirement, all of which are tied to the stock market. It is important that you know how these plans work, as they play a large role in the U.S. economy.

401(k)s are retirement plans offered by many companies for their employees. Oftentimes the company offering the plan will contribute a certain amount of money in addition to what the employee invests. This amount is based on the employee's contribution and company policy. You will not be taxed on this money until you make a withdrawal. If money is withdrawn before the age of 65, you will be required to pay a hefty amount of taxes, which is why it is recommended that you do not begin withdrawals before the typical retirement age of 65. An IRA, or Individual Retirement Account is very similar to a 401(k) in that it is tied to the stock market. Unlike the 401(k), an IRA is not sponsored by an employer, which means you are required to fund the entire plan.

Alternatively, there are variants to both the 401(k) and IRA. These are known as the Roth 401(k) and IRA. Roth plans allow you to put money into the plan that has already been taxed so both your withdrawals and increases will be tax deferred. However, you're still not exempt from the withdrawal fee if you take money out before age 65.

Stocks, bonds, mutual funds, and the like aren't bad investments if done with a great deal of knowledge. It is very possible to make a fortune through stock investing. That being said, we would always caution you to be careful, use common sense, and continue to improve your financial education. As fast as you can get rich in the stock market, you can lose it just like that. Stay alert, and watch your investments like a hawk.

Real Estate Investing

"90% of all millionaires become so through owning real estate."

-Andrew Carnegie

If compound interest is considered to be the 8th wonder of the world, then real estate has got to be the 9th. Owning real estate is an excellent way to build your equity, net worth, and monthly cash flow. At first, it may appear somewhat daunting, but believe us when we tell you that once you get going down the real estate path, you'll likely not want to stop. We are now going to take you through some of the different ways you can invest in real estate.

Buying Rental Homes

Owning a rental home is a staple investment for anyone's portfolio. The basic concept of owning and renting out real estate property is that, as the owner, the mortgage is under your name, which makes you responsible for the payments. However, when you have a tenant, their monthly rent is structured in such a way that the mortgage, utilities, property taxes, and insurance are all covered by the renter. As in any business, we want to do more than just break even. That's why those who own real estate typically charge enough in rent to not only offset the expenses of owning and maintaining the property, but to make a bit of positive monthly cash flow as well. Owning rental property is a great vehicle to use towards financial freedom.

One vital part of real estate investing is property management. You can opt to manage your own properties if you have the time. Or, if you don't want to spend your time on call if a tenant has a gas leak or flooded basement, you can hire a property management company to do all the dirty work. Sure, it may reduce the income you receive from the rental property, but it will definitely save you a whole lot of time and headaches.

Another benefit to owning real estate is that the value of land does not depreciate. Of course, houses can fall apart and break down, but the land you own on which your rentals reside, retains its value. It's not like you can produce more land. What you see on the map is all there is.

Mortgage Note Investing

A note is a legal document that serves as an IOU from a borrower to a lender. When you purchase a note, you are investing in someone else's debt for your profit. Regardless of whether or not you're the one to purchase the note, someone will be profiting from the debt, so you might as well be the one and become the bank. There are multiple types of notes you may invest in, but for the sake of simplicity, and to focus on real estate, we'll only be covering the concept of mortgage note investing.

Mortgage note investing is when you buy the debt that is remaining to be paid on either a first or second mortgage. By doing so, you effectively become the lender, and after some setup, you'll begin receiving checks in the mail from a borrower just like the bank. This can be a viable option if you are looking for a regular source of cash flow but don't want the liability and responsibility of fixing broken toilets or dealing with water leaks in the middle of the night. These notes may be purchased from certain banks and from various private sources.

If you decide to research note investing in greater detail, you may discover the term "distressed." This term simply means that the borrower has defaulted on their loan and is not up to date on their payment schedule. For obvious reasons, these are typically sold at a discounted price due to the increased risk involved. When all is said and done, the type of note you buy will depend on your end goal and preferred strategy.

House Hacking

Another way you can invest in real estate is through what is referred to as "house hacking." Now you might be saying to yourself, "House hacking? That's got to be illegal." Actually, it's not; it's legal, and it's magical. House hacking is where you buy a duplex, triplex, or quadplex, live in one part, and rent out the rest.

What makes house hacking so appealing? Unlike buying a home the traditional way, for investment purposes, a 20% down payment is mandatory. House hacking typically requires around 5 to 10% down because it will end up being your place of residence. This percentage is especially on the lower end if you're a first-time home buyer. This way, if priced right, you can basically have your tenant(s) pay the entire mortgage, which would allow you to have some extra green. House hacking is a fantastic doorway into real estate investing that's less risky than buying a rental house out the gate. It's especially great for younger people who have not yet started a family and are usually more adaptive to moving around.

Obtaining Financial Advice

When consulting professionals, it is important to remember they are human and make mistakes like everyone else, so do not hesitate to take your time and ask important questions to avoid making poor decisions. Remember, you are their customer and have every right to know what is going to happen to your money. You should know exactly where your money is going and what your money is doing. As we mentioned before, the more you know about finances, the less you'll have to go by faith in your planner. At some point, you may even become your own planner. Time and time again, we hear stories of celebrities who make bank, hand their money over to an "expert," and end up broke. The only person you can trust with your money is you. That's not to say you can't hire someone to manage your funds, but you must keep your finger on the pulse of your investments to ensure long-lasting results.

The Way of the Wealthy

> *"To any business owner and investor, you have to be emotionally neutral to winning and losing. Winning and losing are just part of the game."*
>
> *-Robert T. Kiyosaki*

You're going to fail, there's no way around it. Take heart, because failure is the best teacher. The best thing you can do when you fail is identify a lesson you can learn and commit to do better. Although it's not easy most of the time, you can find a way to celebrate both your wins and your losses. While inventing the lightbulb, Thomas Edison put it perfectly when he said, "I have not failed. I've just found 10,000 ways it won't work." When all is said and done, the bottom line is this: Any investment is better than no investment as long as you're making money. You will gain experience as you invest, which will help you to find better investments and get more comfortable with investing.

9

YOU CAN'T TOUCH THIS

"When you react, you are giving away your power. When you respond, you are staying in control of yourself."

-Bob Proctor

WHETHER GOOD OR BAD, ANY LEADER OR PIONEER KNOWS there will be opposition aimed at taking them down. This opposition often comes in many forms. In this chapter, we'll be addressing criticism from both external and internal sources. It is inevitable that you will encounter criticism and other challenges that can, if you allow them, either hinder or fuel your success. That is why we've dedicated an entire chapter to understanding and responding to the opposition you face.

Consider the above statement by author, speaker, and leader in personal development, Bob Proctor. The law of cause and effect states that every action produces an equal and opposite reaction. As we've discussed in Chapter 4, reacting is the mindless, natural way of acting. So, to reiterate the concepts discussed previously, we ask the question, when things get tough, will you respond or react? Naturally, we would want to react negatively to something negative. However, we have the power to choose. That is why if you get a bad grade in a class, you have the choice—are you going to react and get sad or angry, maybe even blame the teacher or another classmate? Or, will you respond by taking control of yourself to use that failure as an opportunity to improve? One of the defining factors between someone who is successful and someone who's not is whether they respond or react to things they experience. Take this to heart. The next time something happens that would naturally bring unhappiness, choose to become supernatural and think before you act.

We're not asking you to eliminate every reaction you have. Nobody can do that. It's not humanly possible. All we can do is shorten the time in which we find ourselves reacting. Regardless of what our reactions to negative situations are, we can all improve and become a little bit better each and every day. The key to remember here is to not worry about perfection. Although being perfect would be nice, it's simply not possible right now and does us no good beating ourselves up because we are not. Improvement is the key indicator for success. Is it in you?

Good Criticism vs Bad Criticism

Not all criticism is bad. In fact, if we are to reach our full potential, it is a necessity. There is some criticism, however, that shouldn't be touched even with a 500-foot pole. If you are making waves and swimming against the tide so to speak, you will undoubtedly face some disgustingly malicious criticism calculated to whip and destroy you.

Consider the source. Where did the criticism come from? Who is behind it? If you think about it, criticism is always given from the perspective of an outsider looking in. Essentially, it's just another form of advice, although given in a coarse and often unrefined manner. In these terms, it relates to the mentor concept of not taking advice from people you don't admire, love, or would someday hope to be like. This may be one of the best indicators of whether or not you should give it any of your time and energy. Let's look into what the difference is between both good and bad forms of criticism.

BAD CRITICISM

This form of criticism is the kind that comes from someone like your typical bully at school, the customer that always complains no matter how much effort is put into pleasing them, or anyone with the intention to wreck you. We get it, it's possible some of these people are just having a bad day. Maybe it's because they got in a car accident or someone offended them. Whatever the case, this behavior is always derived from unhappiness. Anyone in their right and happy mind wouldn't have any desire to make their peers unhappy. If they were truly happy, they would want anyone and everyone around them to feel the feeling they are experiencing —happiness.

You have two choices in all of these situations. You can choose to react to these predicaments by starting arguments and allowing these "critics" to ruin your day, or you can let the criticism go past you like water on a duck's back. It doesn't take a rocket scientist to figure out which one is more enjoyable. Choose to respond by trying to rectify the problem and concern brought up, or, if appropriate, ignore the problem and carry on with your life.

GOOD CRITICISM

Good criticism, or as we like to call it, constructive criticism, is feedback. It's the kind of criticism you get when your parents chastise you for running with scissors. The same criticism comes from your boss when you get a notice for improvement. Good criticism comes from those who genuinely want to see something improve. If and when you acquire a mentor or coach, they will be giving you loads of this type of criticism or feedback. The purpose of all positive criticism is to stimulate growth and improvement. Constructive criticism is often how businesses know how to improve through customer feedback and reviews.

Accepting Criticism

We've all been there; Everyone has been told at one time or another, either in kindness or cruelty, that they need to alter their actions in such a way to either be more considerate of others, conform to the wishes of another, or out of sheer hatred toward their fellow man. Don't take it personal. The cantankerous comments spewed out by another, even if it's directed at you, is not about you at all. Even if they say they don't like your face, accent, or clothes. It's not about you. What they say is simply an opinion based on their perception of reality. It's not a fact. The best thing to do is practice separating our emotions from the situation and try seeing it from a logical, more factual standpoint. Take counsel, and do your best to improve if relevant counsel is given. If nobody cared to listen to the constructive criticism they received, nobody would respect or listen to each other, and there would be no cooperation. Imagine that John Lennon.

It's important to seek to understand one's intentions before jumping to conclusions. It's possible the person giving harmful criticism was raised that way. Maybe they haven't learned how to express themselves without sounding mean or angry. Or maybe you're just extra sensitive. Although proven to be difficult, we ought never to jump to conclusions or make rash judgments of others based on one instance or comment. We all make mistakes and have moments of impatience or frustration. We wouldn't want to be defined or remembered by these actions, so why would we do it to others? Give them and yourself a break by letting it go.

It is imperative that we control ourselves when we face opposition in order to avoid arguments. In his book titled *How to Win Friends & Influence People*, Dale Carnegie put it this way, "You can't win an argument. You can't because if you lose it, you lose it; and if you win it, you lose it." To clarify this point, Mr. Carnegie quoted Benjamin Franklin when he said, "'If you argue and rankle and contradict, you may achieve a victory sometimes; but it will be an empty victory because you will never get your opponent's good will.' So figure it out for yourself. Which would you rather have, an academic, theatrical victory or a person's good will?" Begin now to reduce the number of arguments in which you participate. Instead, replace those arguments with heart-to-heart conversations.

Because it's in our nature, criticism is often difficult to digest. Most of us do not genuinely enjoy being told we need to change. This is why it often takes humility and patience to accept criticism. Criticism can often provoke self-doubt and insecurity if not taken the right way. Lack of confidence in one's ability displays weakness.

Everyone has their critics, but the critics don't have to dictate what decisions you make. For example, just look at any professional sports team. There are plenty of fans that may think and say that they know which players to trade and what plays to make. These opinions can definitely be brought to the attention of a team for consideration. However, all of that is virtually futile, because in the end, the decision of running the team comes from the leaders of the organization.

Another way you can see critics is as simple as the comments section on a YouTube video. Anyone can leave a comment saying how horrible or amazing the associated content was, as well as give suggestions on content to produce. But again, like the sports team example, the content creator chooses to either listen and heed or ignore and disregard the feedback from the consumers and therefore has the final say in the content produced.

As you know, there are many more examples of where critics have an impact, and we invite you to start to become aware of them during your daily endeavors. The important thing to remember about critics is—we decide how much power they have. We can either choose to let the peanut gallery dictate how we feel and act, or we can choose to let the adverse criticism go in one ear and out the other while taking the sincere criticism to heart and therefore bettering ourselves.

The Battle Within

Hands down the hardest criticism to drown out is the stuff that comes from your own head. Some of the loudest battles are the silent ones that take place between our ears. All too often we find ourselves as our own worst enemy.

Many times, you'll hear criticism from an external source, and sometimes without even realizing, you will dwell on and internalize it. This common sequence of events is how we program our minds. Remember, where you put your attention is where you place your energy. When we consistently sustain a thought and corresponding emotion, we're branded mentally, and soon it becomes our physical reality. This concept coincides with the lack versus abundance mindset you learned about earlier in the book. What you consistently focus on will only grow and materialize. This is why if you are to be successful, you've got to learn how to find peace in your mind amidst the war of words and tumult of opinions. There is a beautiful poem written by Rudyard Kipling that teaches this principle magnificently.

"If"

If you can keep your head when all about you
Are losing theirs and blaming it on you;
If you can trust yourself when all men doubt you,
But make allowance for their doubting too;
If you can wait and not be tired by waiting,
Or, being lied about, don't deal in lies,
Or being hated don't give way to hating,
And yet don't look too good, nor talk too wise;

If you can dream—and not make dreams your master;
If you can think—and not make thoughts your aim;
If you can meet with triumph and disaster
And treat those two impostors just the same;
If you can bear to hear the truth you've spoken
Twisted by knaves to make a trap for fools,
Or watch the things you gave your life to, broken,
And stoop and build 'em up with worn-out tools;

If you can make one heap of all your winnings
And risk it on one turn of pitch-and-toss,
And lose, and start again at your beginnings,
And never breathe a word about your loss;
If you can force your heart and nerve and sinew
To serve your turn long after they are gone,

And so hold on when there is nothing in you
Except the will which says to them: "Hold on!"

If you can talk with crowds and keep your virtue,
Or walk with kings—nor lose the common touch,
If neither foes nor loving friends can hurt you,
If all men count with you, but none too much;
If you can fill the unforgiving minute
With sixty seconds' worth of distance,
Yours is the earth and everything that's in it,
And—which is more—you'll be a man, my son![1]

We've pinpointed four practices to develop, which, if applied, will allow you to better overcome the voice in your head that says "you're not good enough" or "you don't have what it takes." These have been proven successful for both of us and many other successful individuals and will be helpful in the pursuit of your dreams if you exercise the effort to implement and practice them.

1. CELEBRATE ALL WINS.
2. RECALIBRATE EACH MORNING AND EVENING.
3. BECOME SELF-AWARE.
4. FEEL GRATEFUL.

The first is to celebrate all wins. Regardless of the size of the win, be sure to take time to recognize and celebrate it. A win can be as small as getting up on time, making your bed in the morning, maintaining a well-balanced diet, starting a business, finishing a book, overcoming an addiction, or achieving the goal of financial freedom. It's slightly different for everyone, but a win is a win, and it's a cause for celebration. By putting this into practice, you'll be elevating your mood and emotion many times a day, which will improve every aspect of your life, not just your studies or business.

The second is to take time and recalibrate each morning and evening. There are two times in the day when your subconscious mind is more susceptible to information. Bet you can't guess what they are? You got it—morning and evening. Take care when deciding what you do during these times. When we use the term "recalibrate," we mean to recalibrate to your vision and goals. Remind yourself why you do what you do and where you are going. It doesn't take long to realign yourself with your goals. It could be as little as three to five minutes. Of course, it's better if it's more, but if you start small, you're more likely to form the habit. Try it out, and you'll take even more control of the thoughts you think.

The third successful practice is to become self-aware. To become self-aware is to become conscious of your unconscious thoughts. You know, when you're in the shower or driving to the store and you don't even think about what you're doing or thinking. There's a time where you go unconscious. Becoming self-aware is to realize when you're thinking uplifting, positive thoughts. It is to realize when you're thinking and feeling negatively. When you begin to realize what you're thinking and how you're feeling, you can determine which thoughts are in line with your goals and which ones must be deleted from your memory.

The fourth is to remember to feel the power of gratitude. Gratitude is magical. If you've never felt gratitude, you're missing out. The feeling of gratitude is fundamental to keeping the evil voices out of your head while simultaneously replacing them with abundant voices. When you feel grateful, you're hooking yourself up to the infinite supply of everything. Always begin by feeling grateful for the good you have, and then proceed with all the good that is coming. This feeling of gratitude will not only support and excel you in the moment, it will attract to you everything you're grateful for. To quote

Dr. Joe Dispenza, "Gratitude is the ultimate state of receivership."

These are but a few powerful practices to implement if you wish to win the battle between your ears. We know the battle is real and difficult, but so many times we make it harder on ourselves than it needs to be. Put in the work and you'll "keep your head" as Rudyard Kipling says.

The Power of Confidence

You should be proud of the achievements you have made and shouldn't let the criticism of others ruin your self-confidence or your ability to be your best self. Consider the counsel of Peter McIntyre, "Confidence comes not from always being right but from not fearing to be wrong."

Every good leader needs to have confidence in their ability to make decisions. As you should know, you do not need to be in a position of authority to demonstrate traits of a leader. The traits of a good leader such as leading by example and giving recognition to your peers for their achievements should be something everyone endeavors to master.

If you spend your life worrying about what those around you think and let them dictate how you act, you'll never truly find out who you are and fully realize what you've done for those around you. The great thing about the unalienable right—the freedom to choose—is the fact that **you** get to decide what **you** want to do with your life. You have the ability to choose the life you'll live, who you will become, and what legacy you'll leave behind.

Why do some people show hatred toward those who succeed?

There are many people in the world that channel their anger toward the success of others. Whether it be by words or actions, they always will find a way to express their negative feelings. This kind of behavior is often derived from something that's been around for more than a thousand years. It's a little thing called jealousy. Unfortunately, it is in the nature of many to show strong feelings of jealousy and envy toward the success of others.

How do you tolerate this? Simple, respond the same way you would as if you were receiving bad criticism, because it's essentially the same. Just like if you give a dog special attention when they bark or whine, giving these individuals special attention when they complain towards you will only reaffirm their emotional addiction to jealousy and therefore reward their bad behavior. This is not to say that you should ignore any and all people. Instead, be smart about who gets your energy. Those with ill intentions toward you are not deserving of it. You have much more important things to do with your life than to give your energy to those who wish you to not be successful.

It's cliché but "haters are gonna hate." Whether you're rich or poor, you'll always have haters. That's just the way life is. Don't let others determine whether or not you live the life of your dreams. Allow yourself the freedom to dream, and make things happen both big and small that will lead you to accomplish your heart's deepest desires.

---

1. "IF" poem written by Rudyard Kipling in his book *Brother Square Toes*. Published 1910.

10

ASSOCIATE WITH GOOD PEOPLE

"Be careful the environment you choose for it will shape you; be careful the friends you choose for you will become like them."

-*W. Clement Stone*

LET'S GET REAL. EVERYONE NEEDS A FRIEND. WHETHER IT BE someone in the neighborhood, a co-worker, teacher, or family member, you need allies in this world. Those whom you associate with determine much of what you will eventually become, and that's why it's imperative that you find friends that bring something beneficial and positive to the table. In addition to peers, people often forget that the person they spend the most time with is themselves. This is why we have dedicated a portion of this chapter to how you can better yourself.

This chapter goes in conjunction with the previous one. Much of what was taught in this book thus far can be applied to what you'll learn here. However, instead of focusing on the criticism and feedback you get from people, we are going to discuss how you can be a good person to be around and how to identify people with similar traits. In addition, we'll talk about some steps you can take to build kinship and camaraderie with your associates.

What makes someone good to be around?

You need friends that love and support you in all your endeavors. Your friends will influence how you act and have the potential to either make or break you as you traverse life. Decide now that you will choose good friends and be a good friend yourself. What makes someone a good friend? Here are some basic qualities/traits that we, as well as our friends, should all strive to possess.

TRUST

Trust is likely one of the most common reasons friendships either flourish or decay. If you want to have a lasting alliance with someone, the first thing you will need is their trust. When people trust each other, they tend to be more open, sincere, and personal than if they barely knew anything about them. The best way to build trust is to show it through your words and actions by doing what you say you will do. Make your word mean something! If all you do is go about spreading lies and making weak promises, you'll find it hard to find solid friends. Be patient through this process as it often takes time and patience to build trust, but we assure you that it is well worth the time and effort.

CONFRONTATION

Confrontation is golden. As annoying or frustrating as it can get, we say it's better to face a problem than to let it sit and stew. Friendship problems can be a lot like the undercarriage of a car that is exposed to extreme weather. If you don't consistently clean it, the dirt, snow, and salt from the road will eventually cause the formation of rust, which will eat away at the metal. Solve your problems with patience and an open mind before they erode your friendships.

SHARING AND CELEBRATING OTHERS' SUCCESS

Celebrate each other's successes. Life is meant to be exciting. There's nothing wrong with sharing your success stories with others. In fact, it's a great way to learn and lift each other up. However, be mindful, as nobody enjoys spending time with individuals that selfishly do nothing but talk themselves up. There is a balance between being overly boastful and selling yourself short on your successes. Our recommendation is to see yourself in others' point of view. Do you look like you're showing off too much?

SYMPATHY

You're not going to get much of this from many mainstream sources as sympathy comes from the individual. A sympathetic friend can make a world of difference during hard times. Find yourself someone who has sympathy, and become one yourself.

The Glass: Half-Full or Half-Empty?

"Prolonged association with negative people makes us think negatively."
-David J. Schwartz

Most of us have probably heard the analogy of seeing things with the glass half full instead of half empty. For those of you who apply this wisdom, you know it actually makes a difference. Take a look at those you have interactions with in your life. Think of a person that always sees the glass "half empty" and a person that always sees the glass "half full." Ask yourself, which one of these people is better to associate with?

The "half empty" person is likely in the habit of seeing the world out of a lens of lack and failure. They may often emphasize the "fact" that things never go their way or that they are never good enough. They often dwell in the negative. If you spend too much of your time dwelling in this mindset and convincing yourself through your own words, you're in for a very unhappy life.

Then there's the "half full" individual. This kind of person sees things from the best perspective. Even through times of failure, they always see the good and try to make the best of each situation. They are always striving to remain positive in every circumstance.

Positivity has been proven to reduce the negative effects of stress in our day-to-day lives. Having a positive outlook on life brings proven benefits like lower blood pressure, weight control, and even decreased symptoms of depression. On the other hand, if you spend your life in a negative bubble, what may seem like a little bit of stress will feel like a mountain of strain. In addition, excessive stress for prolonged periods of time tends to take its toll on us and can weaken our immune system, therefore making us more susceptible to illness.

If you want to know what you are going to be like in the future, look around you. Those you surround yourself with will ultimately be playing a big role in determining who you become. If you want to be positive, happy, and successful, surround yourself with individuals who emulate those traits. Adversely, if you want a life full of negativity, sadness, and failures, surround yourself with people who emulate that.

Happiness Is a Choice

"While you do need people and do choose to react with them, they are not responsible for your happiness."

-*Terry Cole-Whittaker*

This can be a hard thing to digest for many people, but it is imperative that if happiness is what you're after, you take your life into your own hands and realize the only person responsible for your attitude is you. It's impossible to live a life with purpose if you spend your days letting *others* determine how you feel. Despite what you may have been led to believe, happiness does not come from external sources. True happiness comes from within, and it's up to you to decide to find happiness from wherever you are in life.

Too many people base their happiness on what happens to them. Yes, life throws curveballs, fastballs, splitters, and even the occasional screwball. But, just because someone said or did something that hurt your feelings does not mean you have to let it steal your joy.

"Everything can be taken from a man but one thing: the last of human freedoms—to choose one's attitude in any given set of circumstances, to choose one's way."

-*Viktor Frankl*

Viktor Frankl was a holocaust survivor who spent much time in various Nazi concentration camps and lived to tell the tale. As you may know, those concentration camps weren't exactly something anyone should have had to endure. Now, if someone who endured something as extreme and horrible as Nazi concentration camps was able to learn and escape with such wisdom and knowledge, then surely we can learn to choose how to change our attitude as well.

Gratitude

We've said it before and we'll say it again, gratitude is one of the most fulfilling ways to find happiness here and now. The world today often leaves us demoralized and helpless through the marketing of new fun toys, tools, the latest new headline, and more. It often brings what has become a common occurrence in many people: the feeling of wanting something you do not possess. While there is nothing wrong with wanting something, it can be easy to become obsessed with everything we do not have.

Gratitude has been shown to increase positive emotions and lighten moods. Gratitude also plays a big role in the abundant mindset we speak of in Chapter 4. In an article published by the Health Department at Harvard University, there was a study in which two psychologists asked each participant to write a few sentences every week. They divided the participants into three groups. The first group wrote what they were grateful for each week, the second wrote what aggravated them, and the third wrote about events that occurred with no positive or negative emphasis. After 10 weeks, the first group showed increased optimism about their lives and even had fewer visits to physicians than the second group. The first group showed far better results than any of the other groups.[1]

Think about your past experiences. An easy way to express gratitude is by choosing to find something to be grateful for. Even the experiences that you have labeled as "bad," you may surprise yourself at how much good has happened to you without noticing while in the moment. You wouldn't be who you are today if you had not gone through those things and had those experiences.

Mastermind

"Men take on the nature, habits, and the power of thought of those with whom they associate in a spirit of sympathy and harmony."

-Henry Ford

For this portion of the chapter, we utilize the counsel of Napoleon Hill in Chapter 10 of his book *Think and Grow Rich*. In this book, the Master Mind is defined as the "'coordination of knowledge and effort, in the spirit of harmony, between two or more people, for the attainment of a definite purpose.'" He uses the correlation of two batteries being able to power something bigger and better than one battery alone. This example is compared to the amount of thought energy that can be produced with two or more minds working together in the spirit of harmony.

When two minds collaborate in harmony, with a united desire, there is no limit to what can be achieved. We invite you to form a mastermind group by finding individuals in your life with the same mindset and end goal as you. These are those with whom you create a spirit of harmony while maintaining a united desire. Everyone can benefit from being part of a mastermind group. All successful people have a mastermind circle in some way whether through work partners or family. Take the Wright brothers for example. The two brothers, Orville and Wilbur, formed a mastermind, which allowed them to create the airplane, therefore proving to their critics and the world that humans really can fly.

It's important to note that the people in your mastermind group should be team players. The group won't function properly unless everyone is on the same team both physically and energetically. It requires everyone to get beyond themselves and focus on the common goal or purpose.

Networking

In recent years, much of what once was face-to-face has become virtual both in schools and the workplace. Because of this, you may have unintentionally been less inclined to branch out and talk to people. This trend was in effect before, but was accelerated by the 2020 worldwide Covid-19 pandemic. Putting the pandemic aside, we all need to brush up on our people skills and work on branching out. Be proactive in your pursuit of meeting new people and broadening your network of influence.

If success is what you are after, you can't decide to wait for something to happen to you. As previously discussed, if you want something to change in life, you're the best means for that change to take place. Finding your friendship and mastermind circles is no exception to this fact. If you want to buy a car without a care for what car it is or it's condition, you could probably find one within minutes and with little effort. Contrarily, if you want a specific car that is in good working condition, you may have to shop around, and depending on how particular you are, it could take weeks and much digging before you find what you are after. The formation of mastermind groups and making friends work the exact same way. You'll find what you're looking for. You just have to decide what it is you seek and put in the work.

Before you ghost all your not-so-great friends, consider the fact that you can have a good influence on them as well. Sure, you shouldn't join them in any of their negative energy, but you can still show everyone a bit of love. Maybe you are the light in their darkness.

You'll have some friends you can spend five minutes with, some friends you can spend an hour with, some friends you can spend an evening with, and some friends with whom you could spend a whole weekend. Cling to the best, and help those who may not be as optimistic or positive as you. Always remember, people only act the way they do because of how they were taught.

No matter what you do on your own, if you desire to rise to the next level, you've got to evaluate the people with whom you associate. In fact, it has often been said that you are the average of the five people you spend the most time with. What's your average? If it's not where you want it to be, don't sweat it. You can change it.

As you choose to be happy and optimistic about the future, you'll attract those types of people in your life. When you come across such individuals, gratefully receive them. The catch is that in order to be able to receive someone or something into your life, you first must create a space for them. We're not telling you to cut your friends off. What we are telling you is to consider who is actually your friend and who is leeching your energy and good vibes from you. By determining who you want to become and prioritizing the time you spend with certain people accordingly, you'll be on your way to building a strong and broad network of like-minded individuals.

---

1. "Giving Thanks Can Make You Happier." https://www.health.harvard. edu/healthbeat/giving-thanks-can-make-you-happier

CONCLUSION
LOVE WHAT YOU DO, DO WHAT YOU LOVE

"Doing what you love is the cornerstone of having abundance in your life."

-Wayne W. Dyer

WHEN SOMEONE DOESN'T FEEL LOVE IN THEIR HEART, IT OFTEN leads to a life without meaning. Some may even call it lifeless. We hear about rich, well-known people all the time that are downright depressed while they have mountains of money and a considerable number of physical things in their possession from private jets, yachts, boats, to mansions upon mansions. You can choose to be rich, or you can choose to be abundantly wealthy. Some may think there's no difference between the two, but truth be told, the difference is noteworthy.

The differentiating factor between being rich versus being wealthy is finding purpose and meaning in what you do. Another way to say this is to love and be passionate about your work. Wealthy people are rich, but rich people aren't always wealthy in the truest sense of the word. To be wealthy is to have balance, purpose, meaning, and priorities in line with moral convictions. To be rich is to have one aspect of your life in order (money), whereas to be wealthy you have all aspects of your life in order (more than just money). Wealthy people are not only go-getters but also go-givers. To state it simply, the difference is love and purpose.

Our emotions play a big role in what we accomplish and the person we become. From various experiences we have in life, we learn that love is one of the most powerful emotions we can feel. Huey Lewis and the News had it right when they sang "The Power of Love." Love is an interesting thing. When you love someone or something, you have a hard time not thinking about them or it. You don't need a reminder to bring it to your mind. You're in love! This is the concept from which your passion stems. That's why we emphasized so heavily the importance of being passionate throughout this book. This emotion has proven time and time again to have major effects.

Do It for the Right Reason

Ask yourself, what do I want to study? Did I choose my major or profession because of the high salary? Was I pressured into a certain major or field of labor? Or, did I choose it because I genuinely enjoy it? There are many different reasons one may choose a specific field of study or profession, but the most common are money, social pressures, and passion. Obviously, each reason leads to different outcomes in the short-term and long-term results achieved. Let's break each of these down so you can better understand why your reason for doing what you do can make all the difference in the quality of life you live.

MONEY

Money is essential. Just as our body needs oxygen to survive, so too do we need a certain amount of money to ensure we don't go without food, clothes, or shelter. This being said, when money becomes the focus of all you do, you'll never be satisfied with life and have an endless appetite for material possessions. Having large amounts of money is the result of providing a large number of people with a great deal of service. In this sense, the focus should be on providing more and more service to people in place of just working and studying for money.

According to a study performed by Georgetown University in 2015, roughly 80% of today's incoming college freshmen ultimately choose a major based on potential salary and benefits.[1] Although there is nothing wrong with choosing a career based on potential salary, there may be several consequences later in life. Such consequences could be that you lose the desire to continue your current career because you have grown so tired of doing something in which you have no passion.

As demonstrated in the study cited in the previous paragraph, we learn that the majority of people base the decision for their studies and career on their earning potential. While it's important to know how much you can potentially make in each career you research, money should not be your primary motivation. We can't tell you how many people we've talked to who've completely suppressed their dreams, because, in a very general sense, they wouldn't make enough money. Let's get something straight. You can make an unlimited amount of money in any field of work or service if you just do things in a certain way. If you are truly passionate about something, you'll find a way to do it and produce generational wealth in the process. Of course, there is a science to all of this, but if it's your goal and your passion, nothing will stop you.

Pressure

Whether the pressure comes through your friends or family, being pressured into entering a certain career path is hardly sustainable, not to mention enjoyable. As history has shown, humans love freedom. We all need the ability to act for ourselves and choose our future. Nobody enjoys doing anything that they are not at least partially accepting, especially something as life changing as what to study or do to produce a source of income.

J. T. O'Donnell, the founder and CEO of Work It Daily, had this to say regarding pressure to choose a specific career:

> We like to be liked. More importantly, we like to be respected. We want people to be impressed with us. It gives us a temporary feeling of happiness. The problem is we end up making career choices to impress other people so we can feel that fleeting rush of validation. In the process, we lose sight of what makes us truly happy. With each career move, we get unhappier. The more we try to impress, the more frustrated we feel.

It's not bad to try and make someone feel good or do something because others appreciate it. The important thing to remember is to always be genuine and transparent. Be the best version of yourself and you'll attract the people who will help you become the person you want to be. Sacrificing your hopes and dreams for the approval of family or friends may work temporarily but in the long term will surely lead to simply going through the motions with a lack of emotions. We would encourage you to ask yourself often, "Why am I doing this?"

The Dream

What is your dream? Everyone has a dream in life—something that excites and motivates them. If you're not sure what your dream is, then you should make it your #1 goal to find out. It should be something that resonates with you personally and on a spiritual level. You'll feel it in your mind and heart when you've truly identified it. Your dream should be what drives you to carry on in the daily grind because you know what you are working toward. As Stephen Covey tells us in habit two of *The 7 Habits of Highly Effective People*, "Begin with the end in mind." When you start while having the end in mind, you're willing to study and work without pay for a time if it means you're getting closer to achieving and living your dream. Find what your dream is and learn to love what you do because you are working with purpose.

Following your dream leads to higher productivity, increased happiness, and greater success. If you take what you learned from the previous chapters and apply it to this principle we are teaching now, you'll find that you will be more productive in all you do.

If you're unsure of how you can keep your dream in mind, we have a few suggestions for you.

1. CREATE A VISION BOARD.

Vision boards are a fantastic way you can keep your dreams in your mind. They usually are placed on a wall where you will frequently see it. These boards are usually a collage of various pictures and/or notes of what you want to be, have, or achieve in your future. If you keep these things in your mind, you may find yourself thinking of extraordinary ways you can achieve these goals.

2. TELL OTHERS ABOUT IT.

It's good to share your goals and dreams with those that care about you. Friends and family can help you to achieve your goals through advice, support, and encouragement. They can also hold you accountable for the goals you've set. Good friends can even help to lighten your burdens when you are going through tough times. Never underestimate the benefits of friendship.

3. KEEP IT EXCITING.

Life is supposed to be enjoyed. Learn to love life, and fall in love with your future. You are unlimited.

Dormant Not Dead

In the southeastern part of California, there's a place called Death Valley. They call it Death Valley because nothing grows there due to the lack of moisture. In fact, it's the driest place in the U.S. (Figure 3). In the winter of 2005, something amazing happened. It rained in Death Valley! This rain wasn't just a sprinkle either. It was a record-breaking amount of rain in the valley. Due to the unexpected amount of rain the previous season, when spring rolled around, there appeared a vast meadow of wild flowers and grass (Figure 4). This proved to everyone that "Death Valley" is not actually dead. Rather, it is merely dormant, as all it needs to become a beautiful meadow is water. This is such an interesting and beautiful story that applies to us. Take a moment and ponder. Like Death Valley, many of us are dormant. We all have potential to become something great. The more you become your dream, the more it becomes you.

(Figure 3)

(Figure 4)

Nobody enjoys being close-minded. Just like anything else, the first step to opening your mind is recognizing you don't know everything. When you live in ignorance, you are subject to the opinions, studies, and statistics of others. By choosing to open our minds toward education, we mentally step into a whole new world.

Acquiring and sustaining an open mind is refreshing and exhilarating. With this open view toward education and learning, you no longer care what people think about you because you would rather live your dreams than allow their opinions and voices to define who you are and what you achieve. You can do anything and become anyone you want. By expanding your mind to the true definition of education, life somehow becomes more adventurous because you know **you** decide how you want to live and who you want to be.

If you're passionate about a goal and obtaining a college degree is the best way to live out your dreams, our best advice is to move forward and become it. You know what you want. Go out and get it! That being said, after reading this book, you now have a clearer picture behind the formation, evolution, and current state of the public education system in the United States. Now you know what it is and to what you're subscribing.

Remember that obtaining an education is not strictly confined to attending a university, public school, or other formal institution. True education is the art of drawing out the passion from within and enabling each student to feed the fire that already burns brightly inside of them. The purpose of this book is not to make decisions for you. We're not here to tell you how to live your life. Our only intent was to provide you with the facts and various insights and perspectives so you may acquire the education needed to follow your dreams and become the best version of yourself.

Whether it's college, entrepreneurship, the trades, or another route, you are entitled to dream big and to feel empowered and rejuvenated every time you think of and feel your dream. If any of the concepts we discussed intrigued you, do some extra digging to find and apply the knowledge you acquired.

Enjoying what you do is happiness. Being free to do what you want, when and how you want to, is freedom. Let's choose to be happy in the pursuit of freedom. Let's not judge others for getting outside the box and doing things differently, even if it's not exactly what we endorse or would do ourselves. It's time to allow ourselves to dream big and open our minds toward education. In doing so, we will be on our way to building and living a wealthy life.

---

1. "The Economic Value of College Majors." https://www.cew.georgetown.edu/cew-reports/valueofcollegemajors/

ENDNOTES

Chapter One: The History of the Public Education System

Boston Latin School. See www.bls.org to learn more.

See www.matherelementary.org/history to learn more about the history of Mather Elementary.

Eric R. Eberling. "Massachusetts Education Laws of 1642, 1647, and 1648" in *Historical Dictionary of American Education.*

Robert P. Murphy. "Private Education Displaced" in *The Origins of the Public School.*

National Archives. "A bill for the more general diffusion of knowledge" #79

Thomas Jefferson. "Notes on the State of Virginia," pp. 268-275.

Key, Scott. (1996). "Economics or Education: The Establishment of American Land-Grant Universities." *The Journal of Higher Education*, vol. 67, no. 2, pp. 196–220. *JSTOR*, www.jstor.org/stable/2943980. Accessed 20 Feb. 2021.

State of Pennsylvania Constitution 1790 (Article VII, section I).

Cutler, William W. (1972). "Status, Values and the Education of the Poor: The Trustees of the New York Public School Society, 1805-1853." *American Quarterly*, vol. 24, no. 1, pp. 69–85. *JSTOR*, www.jstor.org/stable/2711915. Accessed 20 Feb. 2021.

"Monitorial System." Britannica Encyclopedia.

McMahon, Mike. "Historical Timeline of Public Education in the US."

"America's First Public High School." www.englishhighalumni.org/copy-of-200th-anniversary

Bissell, Evan. "The Knotted Line."

"Horace Mann | Biography & Facts." *Encyclopedia Britannica.*

Groen, Mark. "The Whig Party and the Rise of Common Schools, 1837-1854."

Edmund Dwight--https://www.prabook.com/web/edmund.dwight/1045770

Constitutional Rights Foundation BRIA 26 2 "The Potato Famine and Irish Immigration to America."

"Schools as Factories: Metaphors that stick." Larry Cuban on school reform and classroom practice.

State of Massachusetts archives 1852—Chapters 238-240.

"Progressive Era: 1890-1920s: Progressive Political Reform." Oakland Museum of California.

Dewey, John. (1897). My Pedagogic Creed. *School Journal*, 54(3), pp. 77-80.

Lingwall, Jeff. "Compulsory Schooling, the Family, and the 'Foreign Element' in the United States, 1880-1900."

"Letter from the General Education Board to John D. Rockefeller, Jr" 1902 March 08-Digital Library Listing – The Rockefeller Foundation: A Digital History.

Harr & Johnson. (1988). "The Rockefeller Century." p. 195.

Graham, P.A. "Community and Class in American Education, 1865-1918."

J. Curriculum Studies 2000, Vol. 32, No. 2 159-181 "Retrospective on educational testing and assessment in the 20th century."

National Archives Foundation. "G.I. Bill of Rights."

United States Courts. "Facts and Case Summary – Engel v. Vitale."

"The History of Sex Education." https://www.sexedconference.com/the-history-of-sex-education/

"After 10 years of hopes and setbacks, what happened to the Common Core?" https://www.nytimes.com

Chapter Two: The State of the System

Pashley, Jen. "How Often We Practice." Skyd Magazine.

Stainburn, Samantha. (February 27, 2014). "High Schools Assign 3.5 Hours of Homework a Night, Survey Estimates." https://www.edweek.org/leadership/high-schools-assign-3-5-hours-of-homework-a-night-survey-estimates/2014/02

"Sleep in Middle and High School Students." Reviewed September 10th, 2020. https://www.cdc.gov/healthyschools/features/students-sleep.htm

Wnuk, Alexis. (November 20, 2018). "When the Brain Starts Adulting." https://www.brainfacts.org/thinking-sensing-and-behaving/aging/2018/when-the-brain-starts-adulting-112018

Weliver, David. (Edited October 16, 2016). "When is it Better to Finance a Purchase Than Pay Cash?" https://www.moneyunder30.com/finance-a-purchase-or-pay-cash

"Student Loan Debt Statistics." https://www.educationdata.org/student-loan-debt-statistics

Hecht, Anna. (October 29, 2019). "Study shows financial regret is real—and this mistake can take an average 18.5 years to recover." https://www.cnbc.com/2019/10/29/this-financial-mistake-takes-americans-nearly-20-years-to-recover-from.html

Reinicke, Carmen. (September 2, 2021). "Here's why it's smart to start saving for retirement when you're in your 20's." https://www.cnbc.com/2021/09/02/why-you-should-start-saving-for-retirement-in-your-20s.html

Chapter Three: Opening the Mind

Gioia, Matthew. (February 28, 2019). "Educare, Educere, Explorare." https://www.self-directed.org/tp/educare-educere-explorare/

Proceedings of the National Academy of Sciences of the United States "Active learning increases student performance in science, engineering and mathematics." (Published May 12th, 2014). Edited (June 10th, 2014).

Chapter Four: Wealth Mindset

"39 Entrepreneur Statistics You Need to Know in 2021" – https://www.smallbizgenius.net/by-the-numbers/ entrepreneur-statistics/

"You don't need college to learn stuff": Tesla and SpaceX Founder. Scroll Staff. Published March 15th, 2020. https:// scroll.in/video/955974you-dont-need-college-to-learn-stuff-tesla-spacex-founder-elon-musk

Chapter Eight: Supplementation with Investments

U.S. Inflation Calculator – www.usinflationcalculator.com

U.S. Energy Information Administration – www.eig.gov

U.S. Inflation Calculator – www.in2013dollars.com

Gold Price – www.goldprice.org

Chapter Ten: Associate with Good People

"Giving Thanks Can Make You Happier" – https://www.health.harvard.edu/healthbeat/giving-thanks-can-make-you-happier

Your Guide to Choosing a Major - www.bestcolleges.com/ resources/choosing-a-major/

"The Economic Value of College Majors" – https://www.cew.georgetown.edu/cew-reports/whats-it-worth-the-economic-value-of-college-majors/

ACKNOWLEDGMENTS

We would like to thank our mother who taught us, from a very young age, the value of loving what you learn and the importance of following your dreams. There is no question, you helped and continue to assist us in obtaining a real, open-minded education by drawing out what was and is already within us.

We want to thank and acknowledge our father for the sacrifice and dedication in showing and teaching us the functions of a business and how rewarding the life of an entrepreneur really is. You also made a considerable effort to teach us how to work hard and do a job the right way.

A special thank you is in order to Douglas, Aaron, and Emron Andrew for paving the way for young people, like ourselves, to financial success and teaching us how to attain such heights.

We especially want to acknowledge and thank those who have looked down on us and discouraged us from following our dreams. You gave us the fuel to move forward when we were running on empty. We genuinely wish you the best in your endeavors.

We would also like to thank the composers and musicians who produced the countless movie soundtracks that inspired and enabled us to organize our thoughts and write this book.

We extend our gratitude to the innumerable authors, speakers, and educators that have developed many of these ideas and concepts over time. The world is a better place because of you.

ABOUT THE AUTHORS

Nathan was born and raised in California. He has been studying and applying principles of entrepreneurship and investing since his early teens. Nathan is the co-founder of multiple businesses and is always looking for ways to provide greater service to those around him.

Joshua was born and raised in the San Francisco Bay Area. He plays a leading role in multiple businesses, and is committed to improving them, and himself, to better serve others. Joshua loves helping others to achieve their dreams and find happiness.